Power Against Dream Criminals
1st Printed in May, 2001
Dr. D. K. Olukoya

ISBN 978-35755-0-3

©2001 The Battle Cry Christian Ministries

Published by:
The Battle Cry Christian Ministries
322, Herbert Macaulay Way, Yaba,
P. O. Box 12272, Ikeja, Lagos.
Phone: 0803-304-4239, 01-8044415

All rights reserved. Reproduction in whole or part without written permission is prohibited.

Printed in Nigeria

All Scripture quotation is from the King James Version of the Bible

Cover Illustration: Sister Shade Olukoya

CONTENTS

YOUR DREAMS AND YOUR DESTINY .... [4]

CURSES AND DREAMS .... [28]

ATTACKERS OF THE VEHICLE OF DESTINY [45]

THE MIDNIGHT BATTLE .... [64]

THE NIGHT RAIDERS .... [88]

JUDAS OF THE NIGHT .... [113]

VICTORY OVER SATANIC DREAMS ... [142]

PARALYSING SATANIC ANIMALS .... [187]

PARALYSING SATANIC MINISTERS ... [207]

PRAYER WARFARE .... [227]

DR. D. K. OLUKOYA

POWER AGAINST DREAM CRIMINALS

1
YOUR DREAMS AND YOUR DESTINY

Power Against Dream Criminals

But while men slept, his enemy came and sowed tares among the wheat, and went his way (Matthew 13:25).

We can see from the above verse that the visit paid to man while he slept was far from being a friendly one. It was a visit paid to plant something in his life; and the enemy had chosen a particular time to do this: while men slept. This means that some of the greatest dangers that we face as human beings happen during sleep.

> Why dost thou strive against him? for he giveth not account of any of his matters. [14]For God speaketh once, yea twice, yet man perceiveth it not. [15]In a dream, in a vision of the night, when deep sleep falleth upon men, in slumberings upon the bed; [16]Then he openeth the ears of men, and sealeth their instruction, [17]That he may withdraw man from his purpose, and hide pride from man. [18]He keepeth back his soul from the pit, and his life from perishing by the sword (Job 33:13-18).

What the above passage is telling us is that God talks to us many times, but we do not perceive what He is saying, technically because our lives are too noisy, and this does not allow us to hear Him when we should, He now goes into our dream to talk to us so that, if there is any bad thing we desire to do, he may restrain us from going ahead.

WHAT IS YOUR DESTINY?

Two words stand out in the above passage: destiny and ream.

Power Against Dream Criminals

What is your destiny?

- ☞ Your destiny is the reason why you were born.

- ☞ Your destiny is the purpose of God for your life.

- ☞ Destiny can also be defined as what God has written in his book concerning your life. Jesus said, "the son of man goeth as is written of him," meaning that your destiny is when you go as it is written of you. Which means, also, that it is possible to go as it is not written.

- ☞ Your destiny is what God had in mind before He created you and asked you to come into this world.

- ☞ It is God's pre-ordained plan for your life.

One way or the other, your destiny is already programmed by the Almighty. But then, it can be diverted, destroyed, perverted, smashed to pieces or fragmented. That is part of the reasons you must read this with absolute concentration.

The second part of the passage quoted above talks about dreams:

...while men slept his enemy came and sowed tares...

I pray that every implantation by the enemy shall be uprooted from your life, in the name of Jesus.

Most sleeping takes place at night, and the most dangerous period of the night is between 12:00 midnight and 3:00 a.m. Fortunately and unfortunately, however, that is the hour that most people sleep deeply.

Power Against Dream Criminals

WHY THE OPERATION AT NIGHT

The enemy chooses the night because the night is characterized by darkness.

The night is also characterized by intense spiritual activities. Workers in the dark kingdom are desperate at that hour to fill their quota.

The midnight is the time when most human beings are least alert.

The night, therefore, is a very favourable period for the plans of the wicked. The Lord knows this and the enemy knows this as well.

SALIENT POINTS

I wish to make some statements about dreams so that we can know for sure where we are going and know how to pray.

Your dreams can determine your destiny. God, in His own infinite mercies, designed for man to have dreams. Therefore, if you look at your Bible, you will find dreams mentioned 121 times.

By the time a person is sixty years old he would have spent twenty years sleeping. Since one-third of our lifetime is spent sleeping, it means that a large percentage of our life is spent dreaming as dreaming occurs during sleep.

☞ Dreams are important in human life.

Power Against Dream Criminals

- Dreams are visions during sleep.
- Dreams are revelations of some little portions of the activities of the spirit world.
- Dreams are scenes of occurrences in the spirit realm. The images we see in the dream are transactions that go on during sleep.
- Your dream puts you in touch with some internal security system, with your internal wisdom.
- Your dream will open your spiritual life to you. And these dreams do not lie.
- Dreams are the windows to your unconscious feelings and to your unconscious thoughts. Many of us do not know what is happening in our lives because we do not understand our dreams.
- Dreams should reveal our deepest aims and objectives.
- It is a spiritual monitoring system which helps you to deal with your physical life.
- Your dreams should reveal to you your fears and your hopes.
- It should reveal your past and your future to you.
- Your dream can heal you, change you and influence your life.

Power Against Dream Criminals

☞ Your dream can enlighten you and can warn you or inform you.

Because of all these, dreams are important and should not be ignored. Any dream you have consistently should be taken serious.

These dreams are the invisible tools that bring messages to you. It is your spiritual monitoring system, by which you can know what is happening to your life in the spiritual world.

A brother found it difficult to pass his examinations, so he started praying. Any time he dreamt, he would always see this goat tied to a tree. He never understood this.

He got born again, went to Bible school for ten years where they preached holiness, faith and what have you. Yet, he kept seeing this goat tied to a tree and as much as the goat struggled to get free, the rope held it back. Yet, this brother did not understand until one day when he came to a prayer meeting where somebody preached this kind of message.

He then understood that the goat he was seeing was him, and the rope that tied it to the tree was the enemy's boundary for his life. He could not go beyond that rope nor move far; he had been caged.

Then the brother started praying hard. All of a sudden, his uncle visited from the village and asked to talk to the brother. The uncle asked him whether he recently went to see a

Power Against Dream Criminals

herbalist. The brother said no. The uncle could not believe this so he asked further,

"Has anyone recently told you anything about your life?"

The brother, again, said no.

Then the uncle asked,

"Then, what happened to the goat?"

The brother asked what his uncle meant by the goat but the man brushed the matter aside. Nevertheless, the brother would not let the matter pass just like that. Putting holiness aside for a while, the brother held on to his uncle's shirt, and, shaking him violently, asked him to expatiate on the goat which he just mentioned.

It happened that the day the brother was born, this uncle of his was at home. Through his demonic power he could see into the future of that brother. He therefore programmed his life into a goat and put the goat at the backyard. Whenever a goat died he tied another one down and re-programmed it.

All of a sudden, however, the goat made a strange cry and died where it was tied. It was then this brother began to move ahead. All along, his dream had been telling him that his destiny was in bondage but he did not understand. Then, he remembered the word of the prophet, "My people perish for lack of knowledge."

Power Against Dream Criminals

Your dreams is where you work out your pains, griefs, and hostilities. When something is being hostile to you, you can see. The land of slumber, therefore, is as important as life itself.

SCRIPTURAL ACCOUNTS

There are, at least, twenty-eight accounts in the Bible, in the Old Testament, about dreams.

The first example in the Bible is Genesis 20. In Genesis 28 Jacob saw the ladder.

Then there was the dream of Joseph. The destiny of Joseph was made clear to him in his dream, but the only problem was that the boy refused to keep quiet. He kept talking.

Pharaoh also dreamt about famine in Egypt but he could not interpret it.

Solomon, too, dreamt and God asked him to choose what he wanted. He chose wisdom.

Those wise men that came to Jesus saw certain things in their dream.

Paul, on his missionary journey, saw a man beckoning at him, inviting him to come to Macedonia to help them.

Pilate's wife had a dream that tormented her. She went to tell the husband not to touch Jesus Christ.

Power Against Dream Criminals

Ninety-nine percent of the Revelation knowledge that we need in order to overcome our problems can be revealed to us in the dream; and it is said that to be informed is to be transformed.

Dreams can come from God. It can come from man. It can also come from the enemy.

When the dream is from God, the dreamer is left normal, calm, quiet, reasonable, with open and clear mind after that dream. Also if it is the Almighty talking to you in the dream, He will give you:

- assurance,
- encouragement,
- comfort,
- directions,
- instruction,
- guidance,
- exhortation,
- correction,
- revelation of the future,
- revelation of His plans and purposes to you.

If it is from your enemy or satan, the dream will be mysterious, absurd, sometimes empty, sometimes foolish, and

Power Against Dream Criminals

sometimes leaving the person confused and dazed. The dream would be so unreasonable, most time it would not make any sense; sometimes it is so mysterious that you wonder what kind of dream it is.

It is like that sister who had a dream that she was sitting on a mat while another woman sat on another. Both of them were flying. She was asking the woman in the front section of the mat,

"Why am I on this mat and where am I going?

The woman said,

"When you get there, you will know."

The sister reiterated again,

"But it's not good for one to be flying on a mat."

The woman did not answer her anymore. So the sister began to pray. At one point, it was as if a rope cut in that mat, and the sister landed on the ground. Then she woke up with pains in her back. What was going to happen to her? They were taking her to a witchcraft meeting to initiate her unconsciously.

When your dream is an attack from the enemy, it can represent satanic strategy to cause calamity and destruction.

When you have dream attacks from the enemy, it is for seven reasons, namely:

☞ to steal, kill and to destroy;

Power Against Dream Criminals

- to terrify;
- to inflict terrible sicknesses.

A lot of people wake from an attack in the dream and the sickness takes root immediately.

- to contact a covenant from the devil;
- to deceive men.

The Bible says, 'marvel not because satan himself can present himself as an angel of light';

- to cause man to take the wrong decision;
- to terminate destinies.

Beloved, it is a serious matter when God is showing you the pictures of your life and you do not know what to do. Fortunately, there is a way out because in the spiritual world, you find fast forward and rewind functions. This is not like a physical house.

For instance, as you sit down in a place, you cannot decide to be ten years younger. This is not possible. But in the spirit world, you can do a rewind to when you were ten years old. Likewise, you can do a fast forward to see what will happen in ten years' time.

A sister was praying to marry. She was already 39years old, yet no man had ever proposed to her. So she continued praying. Then God took her back to when she was fifteen years

Power Against Dream Criminals

old, at a particular birthday party. She was serving the guests the birthday cake. When she got to a man, the man took the first, second and third pieces of cake. This made the sister protest. But instead of the man dropping the excess pieces of cake, he drew the girl close and told her,

"You're my wife. If you don't marry me, you won't marry anybody."

That incident happened when she was fifteen years old but she did not know the importance of it until she started praying at the age of 39 when the Lord took her back 24 years.

DANGER OF NOT DREAMING

If you do not dream at all, or you feel you do not dream at all, there is double danger:

☞ If God wants to talk to you, you will not hear.

The enemy's presence and activities in your life will be hidden. Of course, it is that which you know that you would want to pray against. But as long as you do not know, you are in trouble. It is most dangerous in the day of danger and trouble for you not to have information at all.

The enemy has blinded the spirit man and soul of so many people that when they wake up they forget everything they dreamt of. In fact, scientists agree that everybody dreams. The only problem is that you may have the inability to recall your dreams.

Paul was on the sea, and it seemed as if all hopes were lost. But he had a dream. In the dream, an angel of the Lord stood by him, telling him not to fear as nobody would die inside that ship. Immediately Paul had that dream, he rose up and asked people to eat and drink as no one on the ship would die.

If you do not have signs like this as a Christian, you become a weaponless warrior. The enemy has tampered with your spiritual monitoring system. If you suffer from the inability to recall dreams, it is a serious problem that you must pray over.

Very likely, a particular power is afraid of you and does not want you to have certain information because you will act like fire and thunder. And because they do not want you to act, the best thing, they feel, is to make you forget. This is a very serious matter.

If many of us could know what is going on in our dream lives we will understand what is going on in our physical lives.

DREAMS TO IGNORE

Nevertheless, there are some dreams that you can ignore.

For example,

- Any dream you had in a night you were very agitated should be forgotten.

Power Against Dream Criminals

- Any dream that you have when you have malaria should likewise not be taken seriously.
- Any dream you have when you have over-fed yourself also qualifies for neglect.
- When you dream while you sleep in an occultic house, simply forget that dream.
- Any dream you have after a family quarrel cannot be taken seriously.
- Any dream out of the multitude of businesses should be forgotten.

There is also something called 'dream within a dream'. This happens when people have three or four dreams at a time that everything looks jumbled up that they cannot make out the details of each one.

EVIL AND BAD DREAMS

- If you dream and you find yourself drinking dirty water, it means the enemy wants to poison your spiritual life and reduce your fire.
- If you dream and see yourself drowning and crying for help, the enemy is planning tribulations for you.

Power Against Dream Criminals

- If you dream that something keeps obstructing you as you seek to cross from one place to another, the enemy is trying to hinder your progress.

- If you are always eating meat, the bottom line is that you have become a witch participating in witchcraft feeding.

- When you find yourself always eating, and your mouth is even forced open to take food in the dream, it means the enemy wants to weaken your spiritual power and plant sickness into your life.

Some years back, we prayed for a sister who dreamt that she was breast-feeding a strange baby who held her breast with its teeth. She tried to push the baby away but the baby held tight to the breast. She then hit the baby on the head. As the baby dropped to the floor the sister woke up with pains. Before that week ran out, five lumps developed on that breast.

Unfortunately, within one week, the sister died. This was due largely to the fact that despite getting spiritual assistance from some men of God, the sister still went about seeking solution in dark places.

- If you find yourself climbing a mountain with difficulty, it means the enemy is making you toil before you can survive.

- If you find yourself in a traffic hold-up, the enemy is introducing sluggishness into your life, to hinder you from reaching your goals in life.

Power Against Dream Criminals

- If you find yourself nursing a strange baby, or milking a strange baby, the enemy is drinking the milk of your life.

- If you find yourself falling into a pit and are unable to come out, the enemy has imprisoned you.

- If you find the wind and whirlwind fighting against you, God is trying to tell you that there are troubles ahead to retard your progress.

- If you find that your cap was blown away by the wind, it means disgrace is on its way for you.

- If you lose something very important like your shoes or sandals, marital disturbance is coming. You had better start praying.

- If you find your documents stolen in the dream, the enemy is trying to make those documents useless.

- If you find that your clothes were stolen in the dream, this is an attack on your honour and glory.

- If you see yourself, in the dream, carrying a heavy load, the enemy is trying to introduce paralysing problems into your life, the kind of things that will make the person unable to move.

- If you find yourself always sitting for examinations without finishing them, this is the spirit of frustration and failure.

Power Against Dream Criminals

- If you find yourself in darkness in the dream, this represents spiritual blindness.

- If, in the dream, you find yourself being beaten by rain and you are running from it, it means the enemy is trying to prepare trouble for you.

- When you dream and see fire destroying things, the enemy is trying to introduce calamity and woe into your life, you have to stop this.

- If you find that you are travelling and the road is becoming longer and longer and longer, and you never really finished that journey until you wake up, the enemy is only trying to introduce frustration into your life.

- If you find yourself being shot, either with arrow or gun, the enemy is trying to introduce afflictions of a terrible kind into your life.

- If you dream of wearing a rag, nobody needs to tell you that this is the spirit of poverty and lack.

- If you find yourself in an environment with faeces and dirty things around you, the enemy is trying to make you to miss heaven.

- If you find yourself naked in the dream, this is the coming of disgrace and insecurity.

Power Against Dream Criminals

☞ If you find your wedding ring and wedding gown stolen or torn or something bad happens to them, this is an attack on your marriage.

This is one reason why, at the Mountain of Fire and Miracles Ministries, we do not wed people with ring but the Bible because the wedding ring is a covenant material, and if the enemy can lay his hand on it, this can be used to easily destabilise your home.

☞ If you find your keys stolen, this means your enemy is trying to steal your spiritual authority from you.

☞ If you find your house being burgled and your things being stolen, the enemy is trying to introduce spiritual emptiness into your life.

☞ If you dream that a child is missing, you have to pray hard for that child not to die.

☞ If you dream and find a woman shaving your hair, you need to pray for the enemy not to kill your husband.

☞ If you keep dreaming of masquerades, that is witchcraft and ancestral spirits pursuing you.

☞ If you find that you are being attacked by dogs, these are sexual demons.

☞ When you are attacked by cats and serpents in the dream, these are witchcraft attacks from the bottom of the pit.

Power Against Dream Criminals

- If the serpent is biting you in the dream, it is not a thing to take lightly. If you see serpents in your dream and you fail to kill it, you should know for sure that the serpent is coming back to fight another day. If you see yourself being pursued or bitten by serpents, the enemy is poisoning your life.

- Seeing crocodile in the dream is bad because it is the spirit of the leviathan, the spirit that can disturb you emotionally, mentally and physically.

- If you find yourself being flogged in the dream, this is an attempt to destroy your reputation.

- If you find yourself losing money in the dream, this is an attack on your finance.

- If you find somebody issuing curses on you in the dream, it means that forces of affliction and oppression are pursuing your life.

- If you find yourself bleeding through the nose or any other part of the body, this is witchcraft attack against your health.

- When you find yourself in the marketplace where sometimes you buy things and other times you don't, the enemy is trying to enslave you, and if you are not careful, they can give you mental disturbance.

- If you find yourself having sex in the dream, this is a sign that you have a spirit spouse.

Power Against Dream Criminals

- If you find yourself going back to your childhood days, it means the enemy wants to introduce retardation and backwardness into your life.

- If you find yourself dying in the dream or seeing a coffin, this could mean death in various ways: financial, marital, spiritual. It may not necessarily mean that the person will die physically, these other things may die.

- Animals in the dream represent difficulties and problems, so if you see yourself being pursued in the dream by animals, it means problems are being introduced into the life of the person. It is even worse when these animals do attack. For instance, when you see bats and owls in your dream, it means hypocrites are working against you and the spirit and forces of the night are also pursuing you.

- If you see yourself drinking alcohol in the dream, this represents confusion.

- If you see yourself with brooms, it means you are going to have friends who are not united.

- Seeing corpses in the dream are the forces of death coming into the person's life.

- If you see cobwebs in your dreams, this is the spirit of rejection and disfavour.

- If you find yourself wearing wigs in the dream, this is an evidence of fake glory.

Power Against Dream Criminals

- If you find yourself handcuffed in the dream, it means the enemy is putting his curse on your labour.

- If you find yourself with crabs, it means the enemy wants to introduce reverse into your life.

- When you find yourself roaming in the jungle, the enemy wants to make you sweat and gather nothing.

- If you keep seeing padlocks, it means that certain areas of your life have been locked up.

- If you dream and see chains, this means a very serious trap is being set for you.

- If you keep finding yourself always exhausted, it means the enemy is introducing fruitless struggles into your life.

- If you find yourself vomiting in the dream, it means the enemy is trying to make you lose your virtue.

- If you find yourself always crying in the dream, it means that the enemy is planning serious sorrow for your life.

- If you find yourself with rotten fruits or eggs in the dream, it means the enemy is introducing failure into your life.

Some people would notice that whenever they are about to do anything that would give them a major breakthrough, a particular dream would occur and when they have this dream, that is the end of the breakthrough.

Power Against Dream Criminals

SOLUTION

The bottom line of it all, beloved, is this: if the enemy is attacking your destiny, your dream will show you that you are under attack. And in that situation what should you do?

Complete dedication and consecration of your life to the Lord. This means yielding everything about your life to the Lord, totally. Once this is done, the enemy cannot bewitch you.

When a lot of people come to MFM, their enemies follow them and I have been cautioning and warning people that anytime they are coming here, they should know that they are coming to the war front, so that immediately they alight from their vehicles, they should start praying as the enemy is not happy that they are coming here.

You must not be a satanic broadcasting station. Who are satanic broadcasters? They are the gossips. When you come to our prayer meetings, simply face what you have come here to do. Men and women who lifted mountains for God were those who learnt to be quiet; they were not talkative. Someone who is a talkative cannot become a prophet.

You must pray for the anointing of the Holy Spirit to fall upon you. When this power falls upon you, things will change. The kind of Holy Ghost baptisms that people receive these days that sends things running after them needs to be checked.

That is why most of the churches that are moving the hand of God these days are pastored by men of God who got born

Power Against Dream Criminals

again in the 70's. That time, when people received the baptism of the Holy Ghost, they knew that they received something as everything about them – dream life and what have you – changed, and those things that should have been running after them began to run away from them! These people received the real baptism of fire. You must pray for same to fall upon you.

You must pray anti-dream attack prayers that will barricade your dreams by fire so that you do not start dreaming about what you should not.

You must be completely holy. Your level of holiness will determine how far the enemy will go in your life.

As I once said, once you consecrate your life and pray, anointing will come upon you. When that anointing comes upon you it will produce revelations. When you now have the revelation, this will produce direction, and when you have direction success is bound to follow.

At this point, if you have one or two things to sort out with God, you can take the following prayer points. "Whatsoever is strengthening the enemy against me, whatsoever is turning my dream life to a battle field, Lord forgive me today; I want to rise by Your power, I want to move by Your strength; I want Your anointing to be upon me; I want Your glory to fill my life. Thank You, Jesus."

Power Against Dream Criminals

PRAYER POINTS

1. Every satanic bondage programmed into my destiny, scatter, in the name of Jesus.

2. Every dream of failure in my past, die, in the name of Jesus.

3. Every witchcraft caterer pursuing my destiny, die, in the name of Jesus.

4. Every satanic dream attached to my progress, die, in the name of Jesus.

5. Every dream prison, break, in the name of Jesus;

6. I fire back every arrow of witchcraft fired into my dream, in the name of Jesus.

7. Every destiny demoting dream, die, in the name of Jesus;

8. Every dream of the past affecting my life now, die, in the name of Jesus.

9. Every witchcraft and serpent, what are you waiting for, die in the name of Jesus.

10. Every arrow fired against my marriage in the dream, die, in the name of Jesus.

11. (Lay your right hand on your head) Every mask of darkness working against my destiny, die in the name of Jesus.

12. Every power that says I shall not have peace, fall down and die, in the name of Jesus.

2
CURSES AND DREAMS

Power Against Dream Criminals

If you are opportune to read this message, it is by divine appointment. This makes it imperative for you to read it very carefully.

If you open your Bible to the book of Galatians 3:13 you would be in a good position to look at curses and dreams, for it says:

> Christ hath redeemed us from the curse of the law, being made a curse for us: for it is written, Cursed is every one that hangeth on a tree: that the blessing of Abraham might come on the Gentiles through Jesus Christ; that we might receive the promise of the spirit through faith.

The two passages above are specially directed at one of the greatest problems of man; one of the greatest vehicles of tragedies and sorrows.

While Jesus was there on the cross, this issue was addressed. Again, like somebody who buys soap and fails to use it he will remain unclean. We must learn to acquire that which Christ has won for us.

The issue of curses was addressed on the cross of calvary. Proverbs 26:2 says:

> As the bird by wandering, as the swallow by flying, so the curse causeless shall not come.

The above verse indicates that a curse does not fly any how. It must come from a source. If we fail to use that which Christ

Power Against Dream Criminals

has won for us, we do so to our won detriment. The book of Revelation 22:3 says:

> And there shall be no more curse: but the throne of God and of the Lamb shall be in it; and his servants shall serve them.

This means that if there are curses and Jesus takes over, there shall be no more concern. Meanwhile, you and I have to address this killer in our lives. This is one killer that stubbornly destroys with terrible violence. This is one killer that has turned fertile lands into deserts. This is a killer that distributes a harvest of failure.

The Bible makes 161 references to curses. This killer is the curse, and it affects millions upon millions of people and communities. This makes the issue so serious too, that it was addressed on the cross.

Another issue addressed on the cross was the issue of sickness. All these issues addressed on the cross, when viewed closely, are issues that have really down-graded man.

WHAT IS A CURSE?

- ☞ A curse is a force working against a person or a group of people. It creates a sort of barrier.
- ☞ A curse is a counter force that fights blessings.

Power Against Dream Criminals

- A curse is an evil thing around the body, soul and spirit and man's efforts, created by the spoken words.

- A curse is being greeted with failure where success is smiling at others.

- A curse is a sentence calling for punishment or injury or destruction on a person, place or thing.

- A curse is an evil spiritual energy originated through verbal pronouncements. This makes it necessary for us to be very careful about what we say with our mouth.

- A curse is a satanic mandate given to demons to wreck havocs on a person, a place or a thing.

- A curse is like pinching a dog and making the dog to be chasing its own tail. Many run around without knowing what they are looking for.

- A curse is labouring under the burden of backwardness and stagnancy. It is like one fighting against an invisible shadow. You cannot make that shadow if you do not understand it, but know that somewhere there, you are fighting something and that thing is fighting you while you do not know what it really is.

- A curse is labouring under a closed heaven. When the heaven becomes like brass and your earth is like iron and the rains like powder and dust, the issue of curse needs to be addressed. This is so important it was addressed on

Power Against Dream Criminals

the cross. No wonder, when Balaam wanted to curse the children of Israel God took it as a very serious matter.

- A curse is struggling without corresponding fulfilment. You keep trying your best but, somehow, all your efforts do not correspond with your achievements.

- A curse is when your presence generates hatred or resentment. You may have been in a particular place where everyone loved you, but all of a sudden, nobody wants to see your face. The husband that you married who was always doting over you suddenly vows to behead you if you should show your face wherever he is.

- A curse is when your friend proves unfriendly and you offend those you are not supposed to offend. And when you offend your own angels, who will protect you?

- A curse is a person sinking in a waterless sea – he cannot come out and there is no water there for him to drink.

- A curse is a promotion failure, a failure mechanism that operates on promotion. Immediately a person is about to be promoted to a very big position, this satanic messenger will come in to scatter everything.

- A curse is the reoccurrence of evil things in a person's life.

- A curse is to fall under the prison of retrogression.

Power Against Dream Criminals

- A curse is being intimidated and strangled by invisible forces in the journey of life. I pray that anybody reading this and labouring under one form of a curse or the other shall be delivered, in Jesus' name.

- A curse is encountering failures where success comes to others.

- A curse is wallowing in the nude in a dark tunnel without any way out. You know you are supposed to be outside but someone somehow keeps dragging you inside.

- A curse is a sickness that keeps recurring in the family. Some families are plagued by sicknesses like diabetes, hypertension, cancer and such other terrible diseases. This could be symptomatic of a curse.

- A curse is profitless hard-work. In spite of being hard-working, diligent, honest and industrious, yet you make no profit. I pray, once again, that anyone reading this labouring under one evil curse or the other, shall be delivered, in the name of Jesus.

- A curse is the prince trekking on the ground while the servants are riding on horses.

- A curse is to be consistently caught in the cross-fire of frustration and exploitation.

Power Against Dream Criminals

- A curse is being robbed of the blessings you are entitled to. No wonder the Bible says, "Christ has redeemed us from the curse of the law..."

- A curse is swimming in the pool of tears and regrets.

- A curse is falling at the peak of a height from life's ladder. Some people do not fail until they get to the highest height. They encounter no problem for as long as they live and suffer in poverty, but immediately they are raised up, they somersault and fall down. This is an evidence of a curse.

- A curse is having no favour from God and man everywhere a person goes.

- A curse is when a ceiling is placed upon a man's life.

- A curse is desiring to reach a goal without a driving force, a spiritual magnet to pull a person there.

- A curse is not being able to complete any good project despite a good start every time. I pray, once again, that anyone reading this and labouring under any curse, shall be delivered, in the name of Jesus.

- A curse is when you are always looking for somebody to help you without ever being able to stand in a position of help to others. It is time for you, beloved, to say, "I am getting out from this kind of bad situation; that situation is not my own."

Power Against Dream Criminals

- A curse is when helpers have no desire to help you. There are a lot of people who have brothers, sisters, friends and other people who could help them in times of trouble but who do not want to see them. I pray that this yoke shall be broken in the name of Jesus.

- It is when a person stands confused in the middle of the road of life where, rather than going forward, he keeps going backward.

- A curse is not knowing what you want out of life; it is like going to the marketplace without knowing what you really want to buy.

- A curse is an unseen force mocking your best efforts.

- A curse is experiencing a pattern of set-backs.

A few months ago we prayed with a sister who had just given her life to Christ. While she was in the world, she befriended one man whom she promised to marry. At the same time she was going out with another man. When one man caught her with another man, the man said to her,

"I shall have to go to my grave before you will see another man who will marry you."

This was said to her twenty-one years back. She was now forty-two without any man proposing to her since the curse was placed on her. The drama of it all was this. The fellow who issued the curse at that time is now born again and married.

Power Against Dream Criminals

They later met. When the man saw that the lady he cursed twenty one years ago was still unmarried he started praying for Jesus to remove the curse.

Meanwhile, the sister was having a pattern of set-backs. I pray, once again, beloved, that anyone reading this and labouring under any form of a curse, by the power in the blood of Jesus, shall be delivered, in the name of Jesus.

- A curse is the whole universe conspiring against you.
- A curse is binding a person in a cage.
- A curse is setting up the right conditions for demonic attacks.
- One of the major reasons why some evil spirits refuse to leave some people alone is that there is a curse putting them in position. If we strike against such a person reading this, the spirit attached to them will have to go because you have removed yourself from their hold.
- A curse is the suppression of initiatives and achievements.
- A curse is neutralizing the gains of human efforts.
- A curse is a wall or fence that protects demons and gives them legal grounds to operate.
- A curse is that which ensures that at the verge of your success, something always goes wrong.

- ☞ That is why people under curses are always frustrated, angry and bitter because even after doing the best they could, everything still goes haywire. Some even attempt to commit suicide. That is why those under curses are often unfriendly.
- ☞ A curse causes displacement from the place of destiny.
- ☞ Such a person finds it difficult to find a place of rest in life as he goes into terrible marriage, businesses, etc.
- ☞ A curse causes inexplicable sicknesses and death.
- ☞ A lot of people are prone to accidents and incurable diseases when a curse is in place.
- ☞ A curse is receiving the key of failure at the edge of breakthrough.

TYPES OF CURSES

There are many types of curses. We have the curse of marriage failure and poverty. When a man is under the curse of marriage failure and poverty, give him millions of millions of naira, it is just a matter of time before he becomes poor again. Open for him a multi-million naira factory, very soon, the whole thing will collapse.

There is also the curse of destruction, which makes members of a family die like flies.

Power Against Dream Criminals

Sometime ago, I prayed with a fellow who had lost about eleven people in his family between January and February, leaving only two people.

There is also the curse of stagnancy just as there is that of backwardness.

There is also the curse of defeat, oppression, failure and divorce. We have seen people who confirmed that their mother was divorced three times and they themselves are having problems with their own marriages.

There is the curse of family discord, or things always going wrong.

There is the curse of being doomed or being deceived.

All these various types of curses have killed men before their time. Once again, I pray that anyone reading this and labouring under any one of these curses shall be delivered, in the name of Jesus.

So much for this.

DREAM INDICATORS

Certain indicators reveal whether or not curses are in place in people's lives. In Job 33:14-18, we read:

> For God speaketh once, yea twice, yet man perceiveth it not.
> In a dream, in a vision of the night, when deep sleep falleth

Power Against Dream Criminals

upon men, in slumberings upon the bed; then he openeth the ears of man, and sealeth their instruction, that he may withdraw man from his purpose, and hide pride from man. He keepeth back his soul from the pit, and his life from perishing by the sword.

This passage indicates that your dream life is a spiritual monitor of some sort.

There are dream indicators that a person is operating under a curse. For example,

- If you find that in your dreams you are always fighting unknown persons, without victory on your part, you need to pray against such a curse seriously.

- If you find that, in your dream, you always embark on an endless journey, you need to pray seriously, too, because it is an evidence that you are operating under a curse.

- If you find that you have constant nightmares without your dreams making any sense, you are working under a curse.

- If you find yourself always endlessly climbing without ever getting to the top or you, sit for an examination where you write endlessly without getting the results, you must be under a curse.

- If, in your dreams, you always find yourself getting late to important assignments, or just as something good is about

Power Against Dream Criminals

to come your way you wake up without getting it, you have a curse to break.

- If you find that you are plucking fruits from a tree but it is the rotten ones that you keep plucking, this is an evidence that you are working under a curse.
- If you find out that you are always coming back to your junior school or one house where you lived as a child, you are operating under a curse of backwardness and retrogression.
- If you find that, in your dream, you are always slaving for others as houseboy or housemaid, and serving those who should be serving you, you have the curse of slavery upon your life. You need to stand against these, henceforth.
- If you find yourself seeing tortoises and snails, you need to pray.
- If you find cobwebs in your dreams, that dream is telling you something: you need to pray against the spirit of staleness and break every curse of rejection.
- If you find yourself going round in a circle, you need to pray against the circle of curses.
- If you are a man and you find yourself pregnant without delivering the baby in the dream, you are operating under a curse.

Power Against Dream Criminals

- If you dream of seeing a black river flowing, you are operating under a curse.

- If you find yourself in a cage, a pit, a cell or a prison, you need to work against that curse.

- Or if you dream of seeing rats running around you, you need to pray against the curse of poverty.

- If you always dream before a problem, it is an evidence that you are operating under a curse.

- If you find yourself regularly communicating with the dead, you are working under some curses that have been working on your ancestors.

- If you find that you are always being served with a particular kind of food in the dream, then you must know that you are working under a curse of spiritual failure.

- If you find yourself being cursed in the dream, or being harassed, then you are surely operating under a curse.

- If, in your dream, you are always looking for something you cannot find, or lost in a forest, or fighting some giants, it is an evidence that you are working under a curse.

- Any dream that indicates blockages, demotion, embarrassment, being locked out while others are inside, or prostrating before or begging somebody you are superior to, is a dream of curses.

Power Against Dream Criminals

☞ False marriage in the dream, disappointments, crying without any reason, or finding yourself in the graveyard are all evidences that a person is operating under a curse.

WHAT THEN IS THE WAY OUT?

There are nine ways out.

Recognize the source of the course.

Repent of any associated sin. Any sin at all in your life that stands to strengthen your enemy against you must be repented;

Renounce the specific curse.

Revoke the curse, cancel it.

Restrain the evil power behind it, that is bind the demons that are maintaining the curse, bind all the evil connecting spirits.

Reverse the curse.

Replace the curse with blessings.

Seek the freedom of Christ.

Resist the temptation to go into bondage again.

A lot of black people are seating under evil curses issued by their kinsmen, witchcraft powers and powers of darkness. To leave them in place is to continue to suffer.

Power Against Dream Criminals

I would like you to do some two minutes thinking about your own life, with your head bowed down. Are you where God wants you to be? Are you operating below your physical, material or spiritual standards?

Look deeply into your life. From this exercise, this self-search, something must emerge as truth about your condition. God did not bring you here on earth to waste your time. Think about this so that you can know where to direct your prayer.

PRAYER POINTS

1. Every curse hanging on my family tree, break, in the name of Jesus.

2. Every witchcraft arrow fired against my destiny what are you waiting for, backfire, in the name of Jesus.

3. Every witch that comes before me, I bury your power, in the name of Jesus.

4. Every curse of poverty, break, in the name of Jesus.

5. Defeat, I defeat you today, in the name of Jesus.

6. Every invisible power that is troubling my dream, my God shall trouble you today, in the name of Jesus.

7. My enemies, hear the word of the Lord, my problems are over, it is now your turn, therefore, carry your load, in the name of Jesus.

Power Against Dream Criminals

8. Every curse with long-legs, I break your legs, in the name of Jesus.

9. I claim uncommon success, in the name of Jesus.

10. Blood of Jesus, fire of God, fight for me this month, in the name of Jesus.

11. Divine abundance, locate me this month, in the name of Jesus.

12. Spirit of promotion, fall upon my destiny, in the name of Jesus.

13. Every power maintaining any curse in my life, what are you waiting for, die, in the name of Jesus.

14. Every curse of failure, die, in the name of Jesus.

3
ATTACKERS OF THE VEHICLE OF DESTINY

Power Against Dream Criminals

I want you to pray these prayer points before you continue.

1. O Lord, upgrade my power in the name of Jesus.
2. Every internal bondage, this day, be broken, in the name of Jesus.
3. Every pursuer in the dream, pursue yourself, in the name of Jesus.
4. (Raise your two hands up.) Satanic anchor, roast, in the name of Jesus.

We are looking at what I call, "Attacking the vehicle of Destiny."

John 1:46:

> And Nathanael said unto him, Can there any good thing come out of Nazareth? Philip saith unto him, Come and see.

This is the cry of the enemy against a lot of people today. They are saying, can any thing good come out of this life? They express this either verbally or impliedly because they know everything about you; they know your background; your village's history; the founder of the place; your mother and everything; therefore, they conclude, "Can any good thing come out of this person?"

Power Against Dream Criminals

HOUSEHOLD ENEMIES

There was a brother who wedded many years ago. After the wedding, he went with his newly wedded wife to spend the honeymoon in his village, so they moved into the best room they could get there. The room also had a security gate. But around 1:00 a.m. in the night, the brother woke up to discover that somebody had opened the gate and was hearing sound of footsteps coming toward their room. He opened the window in a bid to peep at the fellow but he became glued to the bed!

At the movement of the evil personality, there was dead silence as the noise of frogs, crickets and other animals ceased. Then it dawned on the brother that trouble was around the corner, as the footsteps were approaching their room, he attempted to call the name of Jesus but he found it difficult as he felt his lips were as heavy as iron, then he started calling Jesus in his spirit. Later, the movement stopped by the window and finally went back and closed the gate. Thereafter, he woke up the wife, packed their things and ran away before 5:00 a.m.

However, the damage had been done. I pray that God would help those who are fond of their villages. Not that you go there for the sake of the gospel but to socialise and talk with palm wine drinkers. Eventually, the next menstruation of the wife had no blood, it was rather filled with maggots! By the second month it was the same thing. She went to the hospital, but the doctor told her to go and look for someone who could pray because it was not a case of medication.

Power Against Dream Criminals

The question is, why did a believer who goes to church experience such a terrible nightmare and oppression? It was because there was a ladder in his life through which the enemy came in.

At this juncture, close your eyes and pray thus:

Every satanic ladder hiding in my life, O God arise and let them be scattered, in the name of Jesus.

If you have ever experienced being pressed down like this, lay your right hand on your head and pray like this,

I fire back every arrow of oppression, in the name of Jesus.

These powers know the background of your family, they know that only a few or none have made it, hence they say, "can any good thing come out of this life?"

Please, confess loudly: "I will make it, in Jesus' name." "I reject spiritual anaemia."

They do historical analysis of one's life and they know for example, that nobody has ever built a house and you are trying to build one. They see that nobody has ever achieved a position of influence from that town or village of yours, and they perceive that this one wants to have a different record from others; then they say; "Can any good thing come out of this life?

Perhaps, the council of wickedness has spent sleepless nights to ensure that you do not move ahead. Then, you need to pray

Power Against Dream Criminals

that your God should arise to scatter any evil council against you.

Perhaps, they have been conspiring against you and questioning your life. God is capable of changing your history, He can make His face to shine upon you.

The report of the Lord concerning us says, "They shall see ...", like Philip said, "Come and see", to the statement of Nathaniel who asked him saying, "Can any good thing come out of Nazareth?"

These are the days of high voltage praying, as Mr death is working an overtime, killing people before they attain their destiny, this Mr. death does not joke with people. He has been winning in the arena of human lives from the time of Adam till the present time, he has no respect for anybody.

There is a remedy for everything on earth, but there is no remedy for death, and one of the greatest tragedy is that so many people die for nothing. Another tragedy is that death uses our spoons and forks as his weapons. Unfortunately, death would accept no bribe from anybody. Like I said earlier, you have no right to die if you have not fulfilled your destiny.

This is not the time for myopic plans and weak vision, but the time to mount up with wings as eagle and if satan keeps reminding you about your problem, then you too should keep reminding him of his defeat.

Power Against Dream Criminals

For example, if Mr. Boyo wants to go to Togo, he can get there by road, air and sea - three ways. But somebody does not want Mr. Boyo to get to Togo, therefore, he plans many strategies to achieve this. Firstly, he incapacitates and demobilizes him with sickness and ignorance thereby rendering him unable to travel.

The bottom line is that Mr. Boyo should not get to Togo. In the alternative, he could outrightly kill Mr. Boyo since his objective is to cause him never to get to Togo. He may bewitch him such that Mr. Boyo is totally unconscious of any urge to go to Togo. He could physically hold him down or hinder him. He could attack all his vehicles and render them unworkable, the objective is still that Boyo must not get to Togo.

This serves to illustrate to us that the confidence of the enemy rests solely on the fact that once they have destroyed one's vehicle of destiny, they know there is no way such a person can reach his goal because they have blocked all the avenues of getting there.

EXAMPLES FROM THE SCRIPTURES

Let us look at a few Biblical examples.

Rahab - She was a harlot, but her vehicle of destiny were her hospitality. It was tied to hiding the spies from Israel and the rope with which she let down those spies to escape. Supposing she shunned those spies, that could have been the end of her

Power Against Dream Criminals

destiny. We would not be reading today that she was part of the lineage of Jesus.

King David - David's vehicle of destiny was his divine curiosity, that is, his quest to know what was happening in the battlefield and who was Goliath to be harassing the people of God? He was left in the field to look after the sheep while his elderly brothers went to the war front. But, those senior brothers could not perform on the battlefield until he got there, and of course, the challenge of Goliath was the promotion of David.

Also, the hatred and pursuit of Saul after David was another vehicle of destiny for David. This means that the vehicle of your destiny may sometimes be very unfriendly, it may be things you do not enjoy or dislike in your life.

Apostle Peter - Peter's vehicle of destiny was his fishing job, he did it all the night, and it implied that he was not a lazy person. He was a generous person too. For, when Jesus asked him to release his boat to Him, he did not complain of not being able to catch any fish the previous night. Also, his boldness and humility to follow Jesus inspite of the fact that, at sixty six years old, his age doubled the age of Jesus Christ in the physical.

Prophet Elisha - Elisha's vehicle of destiny was his hard work, his loyalty to his master, his stubborn faith and his vigilance which made him to follow Elijah and get the double portion. What a glorious thing for him? And how shameful was it for Gehazi who could have got four times the anointing

Power Against Dream Criminals

of Elijah. But instead, he collected leprosy, thus putting his posterity in trouble!

Gideon - Gideon, another man of destiny, was working hard in the midst of the enemy, when the angel came unto him and said, "... peace unto you great man of valour ...." He was not cajoled by the angel's statement. He said, "Which peace? when, what I am doing here is in the secret of our oppressors . ..." His openness and admission of helplessness was his vehicle of destiny. His readiness to carry out divine instruction to the letter was his vehicle of destiny too.

Mary Magdalene - What was Mary Magdalene's vehicle of destiny? Her demons of course. From her, Jesus cast out seven demons. So, satan made one of the greatest mistakes of his life when he invaded Mary Magdalene. Some people complain: "If you know the kind of deliverance I have done in the past ..." Well, if such people properly examine it, they would discover that such deliverance may turn out to be their vehicles of destiny. It was the deliverance of this woman that made her to be the first person to see the Lord Jesus when He rose from the dead. Her seeking for deliverance became the vehicle of her destiny.

Joseph - Joseph's vehicle of destiny was envy and jealousy of his brothers. Even his father cautioned him to desist from talking about his dream. He queried, "how can I and your mother be bowing down for you?" False accusation was also his vehicle of destiny. Later on, when he got to prison, he told

Power Against Dream Criminals

Pharaoh's butler that he was going to be released and that he should remember him. But the Bible says the man forgot Joseph in the prison after his release. We understand here that broken promises also added to his vehicles of destiny.

Say this loud and clear: *"My problem is my promotion."*

HOW TO DELIVER VEHICLES OF DESTINY

How can we become an overcomer against forces of demotion? How can we deliver our vehicles of destiny? Because you need a vehicle to convey you from where you are to your place of destiny. For, if the enemy destroys that vehicle, the person will become grounded.

THROUGH DREAMS

We look at this in many ways, by examining our dreams and destiny. In Psalm 32:8,

> I will instruct thee and teach thee in the way which thou shalt go: I will guide thee with mine eye.

It is unfortunate to discover that very few people receive instruction from the Lord. Some come to the church to pick the ones they like in the words of God and leave others, some do not even listen to anything at all. Others are only interested in selling their wares in the church than to pray against the spirit of poverty hunting their lives. The passage tells us that we

Power Against Dream Criminals

should not move if we do not receive an instruction from the Lord to do so.

If verse eight of this chapter is not in operation in one's life, then verse nine goes into operation in the reverse thus,

> Be ye not as the horse, or as the mule, which have no understanding: whose mouth must be held in with bit and bridle, lest they come near unto thee.

That is telling us that some people have no understanding. This is also in Job 33:13-14:

> Why dost thou strive against him? for he giveth not account of any of his matters. For God speaketh once, yea twice, yet man perceiveth it not.

That is, God talks to us and we do not get His message most of the time, because there are so many different levels of communication as shown in verses 15-16:

> In a dream, in a vision of the night, when deep sleep falleth upon men, in slumberings upon the bed; Then he openeth the ears of men, and sealeth their instruction,

In the light of the above passage, your dreams can tell you a lot of things, it can be a source of divine instruction to you for your destiny. That is why the Bible confirms that the almighty would do nothing except He first reveals it to his prophets. This is stated in Amos 3:7:

> Surely the Lord GOD will do nothing, but he revealeth his secret unto his servants the prophets.

Power Against Dream Criminals

It is one thing for God to pass an information like this to his servants, it is another thing whether you understand it or not. God desires to talk to His people, but when He discovers we do not understand him through some medium of communication, He then resorts to seal His instruction to us through dreams.

Say this loud and pray like this,

As many enemies as lay their rods on the altar, my rod shall swallow them.

In every battle that I fight, I shall be more than conquerors.

Through your dreams, you can know whether your vehicle of destiny is under attack. By the time a person is sixty years old, he would have spent twenty years sleeping. You spend one third of your life's span sleeping.

What happened during this sleeping period should not be taken lightly. Because, those dreams that occurred then are visions and they reveal our deepest aims and objectives. It is like a kind of spiritual monitoring system which aids you to deal with your physical life.

Those dreams can also reveal your fears, aspirations, hopes, past life and your future. It can result in your healing, it can change and influence your life. Those dreams can enlighten, warn and inform you. Therefore, they should not be ignored, the only dreams that you could ignore are dreams you had after you had been agitated the previous day.

Power Against Dream Criminals

For example, if you had conjugal quarrel before you went to sleep, you can ignore any dream you have that night.

The dreams you have as a result of swallowing chloroquine for malaria fever or after overeating or when you sleep in an occultic and demonic apartment, should be ignored in their entirety.

Apart from all these, all other dreams are divine tools through which divine messages are brought to you. It may be from you, God or the devil.

A well-read Bible scholar would discover that there are twenty-eight accounts of dreams in the Bible. The first example of dreaming is an interesting thing. Somebody wanted to take over Abraham's wife and the Lord came to the man in the dream, saying, "Abimelech, you are a dead man" He asked the Lord what he had done, then the Lord told him because the woman he took into his house was another man's wife.

The Lord said, "It is because I like you, that is why I have restrained you from committing sin with her. The Lord told him to return the wife adding, "I have told the husband to pray for you for he is a prophet". This marked the first time to find the words, "Pray for someone," in the Bible.

Jacob was a confused man until he had a dream wherein he saw a ladder upon which angels of God were descending and ascending and he remarked, ". . . surely, the Lord is in this place."

Power Against Dream Criminals

Joseph was nicknamed, 'the dreamer' in the Bible. It was his dreams that put him into trouble. Also, it was the angel of God who told Joseph the earthly father of Jesus to take the child and flee with him to Egypt.

This reminds me of a question once asked by a sister. She asked is she should continue to visit her people who are mostly witches and wizards in her village. Or should she still run away from them? God who could command Herod to be roasted did not do it but instead told Joseph to carry his baby and run. This is telling us that there is time for running and there is time for fighting.

The Bible even says further that God can use your dreams to torment your enemy, and that was what happened to Pilate's wife. She told her husband about how she suffered in the dream because of that righteous man, Jesus.

Paul, in the midst of tempest and threat of ship-wreckage told the people concerning the dream he had in the night that the angel of God appeared unto him to allay his fear that no life would be lost in the voyage. Right from that moment, Paul had supernatural confidence.

We need revelation knowledge to overcome our problems. To be informed is to be transformed. You may claim, you have no problem but it can mean three things - the world has given you a 'red card', that is, you have been asked to depart from the 'field of play' or God has forgotten you or satan too has rejected you. All the people of God in the Bible faced certain things and overcame them. Even the Bible says, "Let God arise and let all His enemies scatter."

How then can you claim you do not have problems? The truth is, any man without an enemy is a nonentity, zombie and an unimaginable idiot. It shows you are not useful to anybody. Immediately you make an attempt to mount up with wings as eagle, there will be forces that are ready to counter your move. However, an interesting thing in the Bible is that every Pharaoh has his own Moses, every Goliath has his own David and every head of Goliath has an unprotected forehead.

DREAMS THAT INDICATE DESTINIES THAT ARE UNDER ATTACK

There are twelve major dreams that indicate that your vehicle of destiny is under an attack. Let me share these with you so that you can know how to pray.

Lack of dreams. That is very dangerous because in the face of danger and troubles, you do not have information. It means the enemy has blinded your spirit man and soul. Such people die like houseflies for being ignorant of what transpires in their spirit system. I prayed with a sister sometime ago and when she got home, she dreamt of seeing herself in the palace of a king and the evil king said "By going to that man (referring to me) for prayer, does it mean that the church you are attending now is not good?"

Power Against Dream Criminals

He then told her, "If you go there again, you will no longer dream." This sister thought it was a joke, but afterwards, there was no dreaming in her life again. That evil spirit knew that the best way you can quickly eliminate a person is to withdraw dreaming from his or her life.

Somebody who dreamt of being pursued would wake up to start fighting back. The one who dreamt seeing his child being thrown into the river would soon wake up to reverse it. But if you do not see anything, they will just begin to operate unchallenged for lack of information on your part.

Sometimes, I took a flight wherein the pilot just took off recklessly in the sky. However, as far as I am concerned, I had already checked up my own monitoring system, I got it clear that I was not going to die in an aircraft. As the plane was diving up and down in the sky, I was confident that there was not going to be any mishap, and so, I was reading my book when someone tapped me and said,

"... Mr. Man, what book are you reading in this situation?"

Then I said,

"Sir, this plane will not crash, because I have checked up my monitoring system; if it crashes, you will end up being the only casualty, so don't disturb me, let me read my book."

When the plane eventually landed, he came to me and asked,

"Are you a human being?"

Power Against Dream Criminals

You become a weaponless warrior when your dreams are wiped off.

Dreams that cannot be recalled. That is, some people can no longer remember what they dreamt about when they wake up. Their memory system is either faulty or damaged. They know that they had a dream, but cannot recall it. This is another terrible thing.

Close your eyes and pray like this,

My dream life, receive the fire of God, in the name of Jesus.

There are situations when an incident occurs and someone would say, "Ah, I saw this thing before." Because he could not remember, he could not stand against it to prevent it from happening.

Dreams of retreating back to childhood days. These are the powers of retardation. They are the powers responsible for making a person not to exceed a particular stage in life. When you keep seeing either your nursery and primary schools or the old house your family lived when you were a small girl or boy, something is telling you that you are not moving. You need to wage a war because you are being told that your vehicle of destiny is under attack.

Rags wearing or nakedness. This is the spirit of poverty, embarrassment and shame. When a man goes to school and struggles to study to become a lawyer, but at the end of the day,

Power Against Dream Criminals

all he could afford is a second-hand piece of suit coupled with cheap perfumes they sell at the bus stops, he should know that his vehicle of destiny is under attack. How about doctors without clinics and when they manage to have one, they employ demonic nurses who drink the blood of patients, thus rendering the place desolate.

A person who is supposed to be operating a supermarket is hawking pure water by the road side. These are the examples of what we are talking about. But if they can check up, God would have shown them in His mercy, only they cannot recognize that God has been talking to them.

Being caged, imprisoned or hindered. These are forces of limitation. They put the person in a pit without water. These are dreams of retrogression and of being confined by the enemy. This is a popular weapon in our environment that we must wage war against.

Always dreaming of serving others. In other words, it is the spirit of slavery, the person will always be a servant to others. Many of us do not like the situation we are in, but we are not desperate and mad with it yet in prayer.

Dreams of an uncompleted task . In the case of an examination he could not finish until they stopped. When building a house it is uncompleted and when travelling he does not know his direction. This is a vagabónd anointing. It is a terrible dream showing that the vehicle of destiny of that person is under terrible attack.

Power Against Dream Criminals

Having sex in the dreams. These are dreams connected with marital turbulence and the destiny of such victim is being manipulated. It also implies that God's power is being withdrawn from such life. It also means either partner's potential has been buried.

A man once fasted and prayed for seven days but ended with fornication on the final day. As he was breaking his seven days dry fast, a child of the devil walked in and he capped the programme with fornication! During interrogation, we found out he had been having sexual dreams before. It is when some people have an important business to transact that they begin to have sex in their dreams, such business will surely collapse.

Death in the dream. This means that the enemy has closed the chapter of such life. It could result in spiritual, physical, financial, and marital death - all departments in his life have been shut down. Seeing dead relatives in dreams is an indication that you have very strong ancestral spirits link which you should break.

Seeing tortoise or snail regularly in the dream. It means slow progress, procrastination and all good things are suffering postponement. It is tortoise and snail anointing.

Being pursued by animals or masquerade . This is witchcraft attack.

Dreaming of water. It shows that the fellow has linkage with marine spirits.

Power Against Dream Criminals

If you have been having these kinds of dreams, it shows your vehicle of destiny is under attack. It means some powers somewhere or some human agents have decided that such a person cannot move.

These powers are often successful because many Christians are not serious. They are playing with sins. Anyone who goes to a Bible believing church where they preach holiness and transformation of lives, whose life is not changed, then his destiny would not change too until he repents and becomes an example of holiness. Everybody needs to repent of giving the enemy a foothold to operate. Then, renounce every conscious and unconscious contact with destiny destroyers. Wage war against them.

Let me warn that if a person is living in a known sin and you want to attack destiny destroyer, you will only end up strengthening them except you repent.

PRAYER POINTS

1. Every power threatening my destiny, be broken, in the name of Jesus.

2. My destiny, escape from every prison, in the name of Jesus.

3. O God arise, let every witchcraft plantation scatter, in the name of Jesus.

4

THE MIDNIGHT BATTLE

Power Against Dream Criminals

THE MYSTERIES OF MIDNIGHT HOUR

The midnight battle is reserved for seasoned prayer warriors. Christians who have distinguished themselves in the area of prayer have learned how to convert the midnight hour into moments of aggressive prayer warfare.

The toughest of all battles take place at the midnight hour. Real warriors are known in the midnight.

Let us look at the example of the Lord Jesus for a proper understanding of what the midnight battle is all about.

> Luke 22:39-53: And he came out, and went, as he was wont, to the mount of Olives; and his disciples also followed him. ^{40}And when he was at the place, he said unto them, Pray that ye enter not into temptation. ^{41}And he was withdrawn from them about a stone's cast, and kneeled down, and prayed, ^{42}Saying, Father, if thou be willing, remove this cup from me: nevertheless not my will, but thine, be done. ^{43}And there appeared an angel unto him from heaven, strengthening him. ^{44}And being in an agony he prayed more earnestly: and his sweat was as it were great drops of blood falling down to the ground. ^{45}And when he rose up from prayer, and was come to his disciples, he found them sleeping for sorrow, ^{46}And said unto them, Why sleep ye? rise and pray, lest ye enter into temptation. ^{47}And while he yet spake, behold a multitude, and he that was called Judas, one of the twelve, went before them, and drew near unto Jesus to kiss him. ^{48}But Jesus said unto him, Judas, betrayest thou the Son of man with a kiss? ^{49}When

Power Against Dream Criminals

they which were about him saw what would follow, they said unto him, Lord, shall we smite with the sword? [50] And one of them smote the servant of the high priest, and cut off his right ear. [51] And Jesus answered and said, Suffer ye thus far. And he touched his ear, and healed him. [52] Then Jesus said unto the chief priests, and captains of the temple, and the elders, which were come to him, Be ye come out, as against a thief, with swords and staves? [53] When I was daily with you in the temple, ye stretched forth no hands against me: but this is your hour, and the power of darkness.

Jesus is the author and the finisher of our faith. He has given us a perfect example in every area of Christian living. Specifically, the example given to us through His prayer life has remained the greatest challenge and example for us to follow. His personal example in prayer warfare should be a model to us all. At the end of Jesus' warfare prayer session, He made a startling remark saying, "This is the hour of the power of darkness."

The midnight is an important spiritual entity. Let us examine the scripture concerning the origin of the midnight hour.

Genesis 1:1-5: In the beginning God created the heaven and the earth. [2] And the earth was without form, and void; and darkness *was* upon the face of the deep. And the Spirit of God moved upon the face of the waters. [3] And God said, Let there be light: and there was light. [4] And God saw the light, that *it was* good: and God divided the light from the darkness. [5] And

Power Against Dream Criminals

God called the light Day, and the darkness he called Night. And the evening and the morning were the first day.

Verses 14-17:

And God said, Let there be lights in the firmament of the heaven to divide the day from the night; and let them be for signs, and for seasons, and for days, and years: [15]And let them be for lights in the firmament of the heaven to give light upon the earth: and it was so. [16]And God made two great lights; the greater light to rule the day, and the lesser light to rule the night: he made the stars also. [17]And God set them in the firmament of the heaven to give light upon the earth,

Initially, darkness pervaded the surface of the earth. Later, God commanded, "Let there be light and there was light." In His divine wisdom, God divided the light from the darkness. The sun was given the power to rule during the day while darkness was empowered to rule in the night. Thus, the hour of darkness which begins with the midnight hour was born.

The midnight hour is a very significant moment physically and spiritually. It becomes significant because it is the hour that divides the day from the night. In that crucial hour, two great moments (day time and night time) are divided into two halves.

The midnight hour may appear ordinary on the surface but it has a great spiritual impact on human life. It is the transition hour. It dictates what happens in the new day.

Unknown to most people, the midnight hour is a time of intensive spiritual activity. It is an hour when late workers in

Power Against Dream Criminals

the dark kingdom work desperately and feverishly to fulfill their assignment. By the time it gets to the midnight hour there are lots of unusual rush in the spiritual realm. The midnight hour is the first born of the hours of the day and the night. Therefore it is a period of intensive satanic activities.

Let me lead you into an important spiritual secret; the hours between 12 midnight and 3.00 am are hours of intensive demonic activities. Incidentally, men and women are often fast asleep during those hours. Most of us are not at alert during those momentous hours.

Spiritual warfare experts know that the midnight hour is the hour of serious warfare. Let us look at an example in the scriptures.

> Exodus 11:4-5: And Moses said, Thus saith the LORD, About midnight will I go out into the midst of Egypt: ⁵And all the firstborn in the land of Egypt shall die, from the firstborn of Pharaoh that sitteth upon his throne, even unto the firstborn of the maidservant that *is* behind the mill; and all the firstborn of beasts.

Now let us see how it was carried out.

> Exodus 12:29-31: And it came to pass, that at midnight the LORD smote all the firstborn in the land of Egypt, from the firstborn of Pharaoh that sat on his throne unto the firstborn of the captive that *was* in the dungeon; and all the firstborn of cattle. ³⁰And Pharaoh rose up in the night, he, and all his servants, and all the Egyptians; and there was a great cry in Egypt; for *there was* not a house where *there was* not one dead.

Power Against Dream Criminals

[31] And he called for Moses and Aaron by night, and said, Rise up, *and* get you forth from among my people, both ye and the children of Israel; and go, serve the LORD, as ye have said.

Do you know that the devil's angels that carried out the assignment did so at the midnight hour? The passage shows us that the mid-night hour is the hour of violent battle.

Have you discovered that most spiritual attacks are planned and executed during the midnight hour? The Bible says,

Job 27:20: Terrors take hold on him as waters, a tempest stealeth him away in the night.

A lot of wicked things are done in the midnight hour. For example, the spirit of death has snatched away many lives at that time. Therefore, those who understand spiritual warfare have converted the same hour into moments of worship and warfare.

King David the psalmist, understood the secret of the midnight hour. Hence, he said,

Psalm 119:62: At midnight I will rise to give thanks unto thee because of thy righteous judgments.

To further understand the importance of the midnight hour, we shall examine an incident that took place in the New Testament.

Acts 16:25-26: And at midnight Paul and Silas prayed, and sang praises unto God: and the prisoners heard them. [26] And suddenly there was a great earthquake, so that the

Power Against Dream Criminals

foundations of the prison were shaken: and immediately all the doors were opened, and every one's bands were loosed.

Paul and Silas knew the secret of activating heaven. They understood the fact that the midnight hour is the hour of aggressive response from heaven.

From the foregoing, we discover that the mid-night hour has a mystery attached to it. It is the hour of the power of darkness. The Bible tells us, so much about the powers of the night.

I have received thousands of letters from those who received attacks. Whenever they try to sleep, such people are attacked by the powers of the night.

DEMONIC SQUAD

The devil has raised up a demonic squad whose responsibility is to destroy lives and property in the midnight hour. He has raised up the following spiritual personalities or entities in order to cause terrible havoc in people's lives.

1. Witches and wizards
2. Sorcerers
3. Enchanters
4. Diviners
5. Spirit wives and spirit husbands

Power Against Dream Criminals

6. Satanic ministers

7. Night caterers

8. Powers that summon people

9. Cults and occultic movements

10. Counterfeit angels

Do you know that there are counterfeit angels who operate in the night?

This reminds me of the story of someone who had a serious problem and decided to consult a religious prayer house in order to procure solution to his problem. He was shocked when they told him that the service would take place at 12:00 midnight.

When he tried to find out why the so-called church does not hold any meeting during the day, he was rebuffed:

"Do not ask any question. Just come."

The man had no option than to attend the strange church service at about 12:00 midnight. The man who volunteered to take him there came to fetch him. However, the man experienced the greatest shock of his life when the man who volunteered to take him told him that they were going to walk backward in order to enter the church. The man complained and asked,

Power Against Dream Criminals

"Why should we get into the church by walking backwards? It is abnormal. If someone wants to enter a church he must do it in the normal way. Have you not heard that those who enter buildings by turning their faces the other way round are members of occult groups? I am not going to enter a church building by turning my face the other way."

The man who took him there cautioned him. If you walk in normally you are looking for destruction. The rule in this place is that you must get in by backing the entrance. The man had no option than to comply. He then discovered that demonic angels were in attendance during the strange night service.

LORDS OF THE NIGHT

Other forces that operate in the night include spiritual armed robbers, powers from the moon that smite by night, terrors by night, destruction that walketh in darkness, demonic idols and dead spirits. These are powers of the night.

Recently, a man came to the church in order to undergo deliverance. What actually brought him was a very strange experience. He was relaxing in his room, one cool evening, when somebody walked in without using the door. His sixty-five-year-old father happened to be the strange visitor.

The man who came for deliverance did not know what to do. He simply asked,

Power Against Dream Criminals

"Daddy, how did you come in? Was the door opened? How come you did not inform us that you were coming to visit us?"

His old father equally simply replied,

"Don't worry. I am too tired and I want to go to bed hurriedly."

They prepared a guest room and his father went to bed. Before the old man could wake up in the morning the phone rang and the man who had the strange visitor received a strange call:

"We are sorry to inform you that your father passed away last night."

He could not believe his ears.

"But that can't be true. My daddy came here last night. He is still sleeping in the guest room. Are you talking about my father?"

The man banged the phone and rushed to the guest room. Again, he could not believe his eyes. His father was nowhere to be found. He began to shiver as he had caught a cold. Suddenly, he remembered that he had obtained a copy of 'Fire in the Word'. He looked for it and started tracing our address. That was how he found his way into one of our deliverance programmes.

Power Against Dream Criminals

FLOATING SPIRITS

Isaiah 29:15: Woe unto them that seek deep to hide their counsel from the LORD, and their works are in the dark, and they say, Who seeth us? and who knoweth us?

There are lots of powers that make use of the cover of the night to perpetrate all forms of wicked acts. These spirits can be referred to as floating spirits of the night. They carry out evil warfare against men and women.

They include heaviness, continual sadness, spirit of discouragement, spirit of sleeplessness, otherwise known as insomnia, spirit of torment, spirit of uncontrollable anger, spirit of hardness of the heart, spirit of dream manipulation, spirit of gossip, spirit of stealing, spirit of hatred, spirit of murder, spirit of retaliation, spirit of violence, spirit of sexual perversion, spirit of false spirituality, marine recruitment officer, counterfeit love, harlotry, masturbation, spirit of infirmity, spirit of agitation, spirit of worry, and spirit of blindness.

Do not be surprised, these spirits operate in the night. They carry out their activities around the midnight hour and make men and women to experience strange problems when they wake up the next day.

Do not be surprised when you hear stories of people who slept hale and hearty only to wake up the next day with terrible sicknesses. Such people have received some evil luggage in the

Power Against Dream Criminals

night. Christians who have mastered the art of spiritual warfare know that the best time to do warfare is the midnight hour.

This reminds me of the story of a particular brother whose house was located very close to a herbalist's house. The brother happened to be a prayer addict. The fetish priest had formed the habit of carrying out demonic activities in the night. He carried out his activities without any opposition or disturbance until the brother rented an apartment a few metres from his house.

The first shock that was experienced by the fetish priest was that his clients continued to reduce at a very fast rate. Those who thronged his house in search of some sorts of spiritual help no longer did so. Then, he began to wonder what went wrong. To make matters worse, his demonic tools were no longer working. Surprisingly, he consulted the oracle, he was told,

"One of your neighbours is the culprit. You must stop him by all means."

The fetish priest decided to gain entrance into the brother's room by using the spirit of witchcraft. However, each attempt resulted in failure. Whenever the fetish priest attempted to carry out a destructive mission, he encountered an impenetrable wall of fire. Besides, he discovered that two dazzling swords were in the midst of the flaming fire. The fetish priest was so surprised that he kept on seeing the sword

Power Against Dream Criminals

and fire from midnight to daybreak. Then, he would go back to his shrine.

That fetish priest would have unleashed terror on the brother if there was no hindrance.

Christians who want to experience victory in this perilous hour must learn the art of spiritual warfare. If you want to overcome and experience victory over wicked satanic agents, you must know how to convert the midnight hour into moments of aggressive warfare.

Many of us are enjoying the fruits of warfare fought and won by our fathers in the Pentecostal faith. Most Christians would not have been alive today if the early fathers did not fight the midnight battle.

'Very stubborn demonic powers were dislodged and defeated by spiritual warriors that were raised by God, some decades ago. What we enjoy today can be traced to wars that were fought in the heavenly in the midnight hour. If these wars were not fought, witches could have been flying in the day time. Today, many nations and communities could have been turned to dens of terrible spirits.

Power Against Dream Criminals

MIDNIGHT HOUR AND PRAYER WARFARE

You may ask, why did Jesus choose the midnight hour as the hour of battle? Why did He pray in the garden of gethsemane? Why did He pray throughout the night for direction concerning the type of disciples to choose? The answer is clear and simple.

There are various levels of prayer. Some types of prayer can only be offered effectively around the midnight hour. If you offer the same prayer during the day, you may not get any result. The council meeting of the headquarters of evil would have been brought to a close. What kind of result would you get if you attend a meeting long after it had been in session and stopped? Can you imagine a meeting that was held with its agenda drawn, discussed and concluded and you wait until everything has been settled? That kind of prayer would not be effective.

If you rise up in the afternoon saying, "I command every gathering of witchcraft forces against me to be scattered, in the name of Jesus." Such a prayer point would not hit any target, as such gathering cannot take place in the afternoon. The midnight hour is their time of carrying out their activities. However, the prayer will be effective if you fire it against witchcraft forces exactly when they are holding their meetings in their coven in the dead hours of the night. There would be serious chaos in that meeting.

Power Against Dream Criminals

The best time to attack powers that wage war against you is during their hour of intense wicked spiritual activities. It is very delicate for a Christian to be a deep sleeper. If you sleep until when you cannot wake up even when the Lord wakes you up, you are living a dangerous life. You must get to a point when the Lord can wake you up and call you into prayer warfare.

If God wakes you up around the midnight hour the best thing to do at that point is to go into prayer warfare. God who neither slumbers nor sleeps must have noticed that some warfare was going on against you and wakes you at such a time so that you can tackle the enemy and win the battle. Many of us wake up in the night to cry instead of confronting the enemy. Many Christians hold self-pity parties when they are supposed to be busy launching terrible prayer missiles against enemies and satanic angels.

Do you know that self pity cannot win any warfare? Rather, it arms the enemy of your life with dangerous weapons which can be used to finish you.

THE ENEMY'S COUNTER-ATTACK

The enemy knows that when people attend our meetings, they are given insights into the secrets of victory in spiritual warfare. Hence, he tries to do all he can in order to put all

Power Against Dream Criminals

forms of barriers and stumbling blocks on the pathway of people.

Spiritual ignorance is one of the devil's most potent weapons. He knows that as long as he keeps people under spiritual ignorance he would continue to enslave and destroy them. It is crystal clear that the devil hates seeing crowds of people coming to the Mountain of Fire and Miracles Ministries and prayer programmes.

One clever strategy which enemies use against those who come to our services is to divert their minds away. Can you imagine someone who comes to the services with the intention of worshipping the Lord and receiving his needed miracle only to end up raining abuses on the usher saying "Get lost"! How can you ask a believer to get lost while you are praying to receive a miracle? Why must you take all the pains to come to the house of God only to end up with a fight? Those who fight with church officials and ushers are planting their seeds on a cursed ground. How do you expect your prayer to be answered when you have already allowed your life to run contrary to the anointing which will produce your miracle?

The devil also disturbs people from receiving their miracles by planting those who engage in idle chatter or gossips to surround them. You must watch what you do during the day. If you have a bad day, you might have a bad night. If you have a bad night, you might have a bad day. Therefore, you must ensure that your day and your night are converted to weapons of spiritual victory.

From the foregoing we have discovered that to pray during the midnight hour is to meet the enemy at the place of battle. Terrible problems that are coming against us are programmed and executed mostly at night. What comes into manifestation during the day are generally programmed in the spiritual realm during the night.

The enemy often tries to affect our sub-conscious mind when his attempts at attacking the conscious are thwarted. When the devil discovers that he often gets no where when he attacks you physically, he would try to attack you in the night. That is why Jesus stated that the enemy does a lot of havoc when men are asleep.

> Matthew 13:24-26: Another parable put he forth unto them, saying, The kingdom of heaven is likened unto a man which sowed good seed in his field: [25]But while men slept, his enemy came and sowed tares among the wheat, and went his way. [26]But when the blade was sprung up, and brought forth fruit, then appeared the tares also.

SPIRITUAL ENGINEERING

An understanding of the spiritual mechanism which the devil uses is crucial to your victory. What satanic agents or demons scheme and programme during the night is carried out during

Power Against Dream Criminals

the day. When evil instructions are passed against you in the night, evil messengers will go ahead to carry them out at the day time.

Here is a very strong spiritual principle, 'paralyse satanic agents in the night and you will render them inactive during the day.' If you stop satanic coups in the night, they will not be able to carry it out during the day. Hence, you can stop all satanic coups against your life by engaging in spiritual warfare in the midnight hour.

The midnight prayer is the mystery of survival.

Midnight prayer is so power packed that it will achieve outstanding results when other forms of prayer fail. This kind of prayer can hardly be compared with other types of prayer. When you send prayer arrows against wicked forces during the night hour, it would enter the heart of the enemy.

This may surprise you; a lot of demons take their rest during the day while they become active when men are asleep. I am yet to see a Christian with an outstanding testimony who experienced a breakthrough without taking his battle into the midnight hour. If you bind such powers during the day, you are wasting both your time and your prayer efforts.

Recently, I gave a particular brother some prayer points at the instance of my ministerial visit to our branch in Port Harcourt, Nigeria. I specifically instructed the brother to carry out the prayer points during the hours of 11:00pm and 3:00am.

Power Against Dream Criminals

The brother had not handled that kind of warfare prayer before. He had been an old time Christian. He was worshipping in another church before he got to know about what God is doing in this ministry and decided to come for help.

As soon as he started the first prayer point, all the dogs in the neighbourhood erupted with a cacophony of howling and barking which lasted till day break. The more he prayed, the more the dogs continued to bark and howl. Then it dawned on him that he has sparked up trouble in the spiritual realm. He wanted to find out what was really happening. He decided not to handle the prayer points the next day. Strange enough, none of the dogs barked.

The following day, he got up at the midnight hour and began to pray the prayer points. He was shocked when the dogs began to bark. Again, the dogs barked from dawn till the next day. At that point, the brother became afraid. He was visibly shaken. He then discovered that there must have been serious traffic in that community.

God expects us to offer the midnight hour as a sacrifice unto Him. Jesus said, "Can you not watch with me for one hour?" The moment you programme your prayer into the night, the Lord will continue to wake you up every night.

Do you know that members of the occult and cults carry out their important activities during the day and they make use of the hour of the night to evaluate what they achieved in the spiritual realm during the preceding night?

Power Against Dream Criminals

The best time to catch a thief is during the act.

Demonic powers are best confronted and conquered during the hours of the night.

Do you know that things like cats, birds and owls make sounds in the night because they are creatures of the night?

At this point I want you to pray this prayer point with every spiritual energy within you:

Any evil bird making evil noise around my place of residence, I command the ground to swallow you, in the name of Jesus.

When you start a night watch with the Lord your life will no longer be the same. It is unfortunate, however, that many Christians participate in or carry out night vigils because they are compelled by situations or circumstances. God is happier with us when we get involved with midnight battles.

The midnight hour or the night is the best time to come against wicked spiritual forces as well as against their respective meeting places. There must be consistency on your part. Some Christians hold night vigils once in six months while they allow the devil to gather momentum and attack them.

Power Against Dream Criminals

WHAT THE MIDNIGHT HOUR IS FOR

The midnight hour is the time to counter and destroy any evil altar that has been raised up against you.

The midnight hour is the time to recall and break all incantations uttered against you.

The midnight hour is the time to ask the enemy to leave you.

Interestingly, it is the time to make those who are owing you to pay.

Do you know that there are many people in many cities that deny themselves of sleep during the night? Such people go to cemeteries and other places of power in order to destroy human life. Such people tidy up their deals with the devil in the hours of the night.

Do you know that those who understand the mystery of midnight hour do not make empty boast? When they come up with threats, they go ahead to effect it during the hours of the night.

The head of a very powerful witchcraft society once threatened a man of God. This man said,

"As the head of this witchcraft organisation, I hereby declare that you will die in seven days."

Immediately he made the pronouncement the witchcraft personality followed up with action by having several sleepless

Power Against Dream Criminals

nights during which he tabled the man of God's case in their witchcraft society. Thank God, the Pastor has also learned the secret of warfare in the night. The man of God also kept vigil several nights. His prayer point and proclamation every night was "As the Lord liveth and the Holy spirit liveth it shall be unto the man according to the word of his own mouth. The God that answereth by fire let him be God. O Lord, answer by fire and disgrace the evil messenger. I will not die by the grace of God. If you are God, let his sentence follow him, in Jesus' name."

That was how the man of God prayed. On the seventh day, the head of the witchcraft society was busy with a cup of tea when worms began to come out of his body. That was how the satanic agent met his waterloo.

I feel sorry for Christians who go to bed by 8.pm or 9p.m and never wake up till 8 o'clock the next day. You must do whatever you can do in order to observe night vigil. You may not have to do night vigil every night but you can easily programme midnight prayer into your life on regular basis.

HOW THEN CAN WE CULTIVATE THE HABIT OF PRAYING THE MIDNIGHT HOUR?

- Desire it
- Determine to purse it
- Practicalise it
- Know the kind of prayer to pray

If you want to know the type of prayer to pray, you can use our prayer manual: Pray Your Way to Breakthroughs, Prayer Rain, and Violent Prayers to Disgrace Stubborn Problems. For example, if you want to handle prayer points titled the Aggressive Prayer of the Psalmist, the best hour is between 12 midnight and 3:00am. Prayer Against Household Wickedness can also be handled in the night. You can release confusion into the camp of your enemies. You must get involved in the midnight battle. You must understand the mystery of the night and get involved in the greatest battle of all times - THE MIDNIGHT BATTLE.

PRAYER POINTS

1. Where others have failed, I shall succeed by fire, in the name of Jesus.

Power Against Dream Criminals

2. The moon shall not smite me by night, in the name of Jesus.

3. Every evil bird targeted against my destiny, fall down and die, in the name of Jesus.

4. You the power of the night working against my life, die in the name of Jesus.

5. You the power of the night operating between 1:00 am to 2:00 am, I bury you alive, in the name of Jesus.

6. You the power of the night between 2:00 am to 3:00 am, I bury you alive, in the name of Jesus.

7. Let God arise and let all my enemies be scattered, in the name of Jesus.

5
THE NIGHT RAIDERS

Power Against Dream Criminals

There is an important aspect of spiritual warfare which has been neglected by the global company of prayer warriors.

Many prayer warriors have not been able to deal with powers that attack men and women in the night.

People have suffered terrible problems and received greatest attacks at night. A lot of people who were healthy, happy, sound and normal went to bed in the night only to wake up with mysterious sicknesses, mental disorder, business failure, death of a loved one, collapse of marital relationships and other mishaps.

Unless you learn how to deal with night raiders, you will continue to go through some problems in life. The believers who know how to target and deal with these wicked night raiders will recognise that the root or the foundation of the problem will begin to shake. Evil powers will no longer be able to hold sway over your life. Satan's arrow will no longer penetrate your life. Long-standing problems will vanish and things that appear impossible in your life will become possible.

The average Christian loves peace. Most Christians preoccupy themselves with seeking and pursuing peace. Nobody wants conflicts and hostilities. Most of us would like to go through a whole year without a single attack. That is a dream that will never come to pass. Whether we like it or not the devil has declared war against every one of us.

Power Against Dream Criminals

Every believer is in the battle field. To choose to fold your hands is to decide to become a casualty on the field. Even if you are not conscious of the fact that you are on the battle field, that does not exempt you from the warfare. Satan hates every one of us with perfect hatred. He is active every minute, fighting to destroy everyone who has relationship with God. You owe yourself the duty of fighting the battles of life and dealing with every attack that comes your way, either in the day or at night.

The activities of evil night raiders are exposed in four passages in the Scriptures. These passages unravel the mystery, the secrets, the strength and the weaknesses of wicked night raiders.

> Matthew 13:25: But while men slept, his enemy came and sowed tares among the wheat, and went his way.

Sleep is a very strong friend of the enemy. He has specialised in using sleep as a form of anaesthesia to perform evil operations on innocent men and women. He makes use of the cover of darkness as a cloak for attacking his victims. He attacks people where they are weak, vulnerable and unprotected. He is conscious of the fact that the moment a person goes to bed he becomes unconscious and unable to resist attacks. That is why 90 per cent of the attacks which people go through occur in the night.

> Have respect unto the covenant: for the dark places of the earth are full of the habitations of cruelty (Psalm 74:20).

Power Against Dream Criminals

This second passage is quite revealing. Here, reference is made to a realm that is hidden from human view, the dark places of the earth. This hidden realm is the habitation of wicked forces which operate in the night. The Bible makes it very clear that members of that evil society are cruel. Everything they do has a tincture of cruelty. Anything they do against individuals in the night is cruel and wicked.

There are regions of the universe which cannot be seen with our naked eyes. In parts of that invisible realm, lots of activities are carried out with the intent of unleashing cruelty upon men and women.

The dark places of the earth are found in every community. The community in which you live is filled with invisible powers whose task is to wait for the hour of darkness and attack men, women and children. For someone to become a member of that society, he or she must be a wicked person.

The Bible gives a vivid picture of some of the activities that take place in dark places in Job 4:12-14:

> Now a thing was secretly brought to me, and mine ear received a little thereof. In thoughts from the visions of the night, when deep sleep falleth on men, Fear came upon me, and trembling, which made all my bones to shake. Then a spirit passed before my face; the hair of my flesh stood up:

Job was attacked by a night visitor. Job did not bargain for what happened to him. All he wanted was sleep but he woke up the next day trembling and fearful. A spirit visited him. This

Power Against Dream Criminals

made his hair to stand on end. That experience was embarrassing to him. The attack was so vivid that he trembled when he woke up.

We are given further insights into the activities of night raiders in Eph. 5:11:

> And have no fellowship with the unfruitful works of darkness, but rather reprove them.

In this passage, emphasis is placed on what is done under the cover of darkness. The Bible says that those things are so bad that it is improper to speak about them. What evil powers do in secret s terrible. Only God can open our eyes to the reality of what happens in the spiritual realm.

Satanic night raiders have destroyed so many lives. It is nice when you are able to build walls around your house and put broken bottles or barbed wires on it. That is a very good effort. These satanic raiders do not need the doors of their victims opene to carry out their activities. They can go in and out of walls. They carry out their activities at all times and in all places, even when serious efforts are made to ensure security.

A friend of mine happened to be a senior military officer. In spite of all the efforts I made to share the gospel with him, he decided not to give his life to Christ. However, he was jolted out of his complacent state when he had a strange experience. He was sitting in his office one day, when a strange visitor entered, beating all security efforts put in place by this high ranking military officer. The strange visitor held his shirt and said: "Tell

Power Against Dream Criminals

me, don't you know that I can kill you right now? Where are your body guards?" The military officer was thrown into confusion. The strange visitor spent a minute or two and went out.

The military officer felt that his body guards were careless and decided to charge them for dereliction of duty. He summoned all of them and the personal security staff and queried:

"Why did you allow that man to pass through the security post my office?"

They wondered what the officer was saying. They told him that no human being passed through the security department. Again, he told them:

"But the man left my office right now. Didn't you see him when he was coming out?"

They answered him:

"Sir, we are always standing at attention. It is impossible for any man to beat our security check point and come into your office. Nobody passed through this place."

He could not believe them.

He told them again:

"But the man came inside and spoke face to face with me."

All the soldiers stood their ground saying:

Power Against Dream Criminals

"Sir, that can never happen. Nobody can ever pass through this check point. It is impossible."

It then dawned on the senior military officer that he had received a different kind of visitor. From that day, he gave his life to Christ and committed himself unto the only One who neither slumbers nor sleeps.

You have lots of invisible enemies who do not need to take permission from you before attempting to attack you. They operate under the cover of darkness. Unfortunately, you cannot see them, neither can you detect their activities. That is why I want you to close your eyes right now and take this prayer point:

Oh Lord, open my spiritual eyes, in the name of Jesus.

There is a testimony in one of our booklets, Power Must Change Hands, concerning a woman. The woman had a friend whom she thought was a true friend. The woman dreamt of a cow coming to attack her in her dream and decided to share that dream with the close friend, who opted to take her to a particular man of God. The woman was surprised by what the man of God said. Instead of saying anything to the woman who had the dreams, the pastor faced the friend who brought her and said:

"Let me warn you, you must stop your evil work. If you attack her again, God will deal with you."

Her friend simply said:

Power Against Dream Criminals

"Yes sir, I have noted what you said, I will comply."

The woman kept on praying asking God to intervene in her situation. One night, the cow came as usual to attack her. However, the woman had learnt to pray fervently. Her prayer point before she slept that night was: "Let the Rock of ages smash my opposition."

Just as the cow was about to hit the woman, a mighty rock came between her and the cow. And the cow crashed on the rock, fell down and died instantly. Early the next morning, neighbours came knocking at her door to tell her that her friend died that night. They also told her that there was a very big wound on the head of her friend, as if someone had hit her with a big stone. That was how God gave the woman victory over her unfriendly friend.

Once again I want you to close your eyes and take this prayer point:

Oh Lord, open my spiritual eyes, in the name of Jesus.

A friend of mine had a very strange experience when he imported some goods. One of the items disappeared mysteriously. He ransacked everywhere but could not find the item. But God gave him a revelation after he had prayed. As he slept, God took him to one of the warehouses at the seaport. God told him: "Go to the left, to the right and to the left again and look under a particular table."

Power Against Dream Criminals

He did and to his surprise, he found the missing item there. When he woke up, he went to the office of the clearing agents and boldly asked them: "Where is the missing item?" They told him that they had tried their best but could not find it. He told the agents that the good was in one of the warehouses and that he knew the particular spot where it was.

They laughed at him saying:

"What are you trying to say? We have not found the missing item. We have tried our best. The item is nowhere to be found."

He insisted that if they would allow him, he would fetch the item from where it was hidden. The clearing agents flared up saying,

"Are you trying to say that we have stolen your item? We have told you that the item is nowhere to be found. Now, we are going to allow you to search for it but if you cannot find it, we are going to prosecute you for libel."

The man told them that they should prosecute him if he failed to bring the item from where it was hidden. The man was so bold because God had given him a clear revelation.

The brother asked the clearing agents to follow him as he followed exactly the same direction given to him in the dream. He turned to the left, to the right and to the left again and behold, there was a table. He bent down and brought out his item. It was hidden there by someone who stole it and wanted

Power Against Dream Criminals

to take it away when nobody would be around. All the clearing agents were embarrassed.

Another friend of mine also had a strange experience when he decided to hire new staff. Twelve people turned up for the interview. My friend had soaked himself in prayer before the day of the interview and God opened his eyes to see beyond the physical realm. To his surprise, he saw the applicants in very strange postures. Some of them were sitting on their heads, others were hanging in the air while some were hiding under the table.

Out of the twelve people, only one was free spiritually. He quickly decided to cancel the interview. "Gentlemen, this interview has been cancelled due to certain reasons beyond our control. You are free to go back home. Just leave your addresses behind and we shall get in touch with you if necessary."

As people were going out one by one, he pulled the coat of the only one who was spiritually free and told him to wait behind for a brief chat. He later interviewed him and decided to employ him. That was how God saved him from employing wizards who would have ruined his new company.

Several years ago, when I was a young Christian, I had an unusual experience. A creature that looked like a gorilla appeared beside my window. I thought I was dreaming, opened my eyes and the gorilla was there. I closed my eyes and it was still there. Then it became clear to me that a night raider had come to visit me.

Power Against Dream Criminals

The creature opened his mouth to announce where it came from. Then I went into an aggressive prayer session and the evil creature disappeared.

That was how I dealt with that evil night raider.

You must close your eyes at this moment and take this prayer point:

Every night raider, be disgraced, in the name of Jesus.

Did you take that prayer point? I want you to repeat it now with some slight variation:

Every night raider, be disgraced right now, in the name of Jesus.

WHY NIGHT RAIDERS OPERATE IN THE NIGHT

Night raiders carry out all their activities in the night because darkness provides a good cover for their evil activities. It is clear that the night is characterised by darkness. Here are the characteristics of darkness.

Darkness is the absence of light.

Darkness is not a positive creation. It is the consequence of the absence of the sun.

Power Against Dream Criminals

Darkness is the result of obscuring light. It comes up when light is hindered from penetrating into a particular place.

People find darkness uncomfortable because of the uncertainty of the environment where it is.

Darkness can cause a person to lose his way.

Darkness can make a person to expose himself unconsciously to danger. For example, if there is a snake in a dark room which you cannot see, you will expose yourself to danger.

Darkness causes a person to wander about.

Darkness causes an individual to stumble. Men easily stumble when they find themselves in darkness. That is why the Bible says: "Give glory to the Lord your God, before he calls darkness and before your feet stumble upon the dark mountains, and while you look for light he turned it to the shadow of death and made it gross darkness" (Jeremiah 13:16).

There are degrees of darkness - We have partial darkness, medium darkness and gross darkness. For example, if you decide to illuminate a large building with one candle, you will have partial darkness, but if there is no light there at all you will have total darkness.

Darkness is silent - There is a lot of silence in dark places.

Power Against Dream Criminals

Darkness has a binding power - It binds people and limits their activities. Whenever there is darkness, you are confused. You do not know where or how far you can go.

Darkness has separating power - The introduction of darkness causes division.

Sleep takes place mostly at night. At that time, every evil takes place. Your best friend may turn around to harm you under the cover of darkness. The devil has released an army of night raiders upon the sons of men. The night is the most conducive time for evil powers to carry out their evil activities. A lot of evil things take place at night.

Sacrifices, robbery, witchcraft attacks, demonic meetings, disco parties and other evil things take place at night. If you have observed properly, you would have observed that most of the things which people find difficult to do during the day are done in the night. If you survey all the evil activities that are done in your community, you will observe that most of them are carried out in the night.

This shows that the night is meant for works of darkness. Most drinking places, drug joints, disco houses and other places where men and women carry out nefarious activities are generally active in the night. I hope there is no true believer who runs a beer parlour. Anyone who does that and calls himself or herself a believer is living in self deceit. Any believer who sells alcoholic drinks is also joking with hell fire.

Power Against Dream Criminals

Most criminals go about in the dark hours of the night. Most witchcraft meetings are held at night. Generally speaking, iniquity flourishes in the night.

WHO THE NIGHT RAIDERS ARE

Marine powers - They carry out their activities in the night. Many of them are found in the streets at night. They roam the streets as ladies looking for men who will give them lift. Unfortunately, some foolish men enter their traps, not knowing that they are carrying strange entities to their homes.

When a single lady who is below 25 decides to stand alone under a dark bridge at about 1:00 a.m., looking for a lift, she cannot be an ordinary person. An intelligent man should know that a lady must have some extra powers for her to stand there alone without fear at that time of the night. She must be a creature of the night herself.

Something usually happens during some night parties. The moment it is mid-night, some extremely and unnaturally beautiful ladies appear at such parties. It is often difficult to identify them. They come in without being invited. Some men quickly rush to them not knowing that they are delegates from the marine world. They are part of the company of the evil night raiders.

Familiar spirits - These forces go about confusing men and women, causing disasters, initiating people, distorting people's

Power Against Dream Criminals

lives, causing demotion and fuelling the power of household wickedness. The strength of these powers lies in the fact that they are thoroughly familiar with their victims. They are able to carry out their evil activities because the secrets of their victims are known to them.

Witchcraft powers - These powers are well-known to Africans. Although witches and wizards are somehow active during the day, they carry out most of their activities during the night. The hours of the night are their finest moment. As men and women lay down their weary bodies, witchcraft powers settle down to work by destroying lives and property.

Forest demons - These powers sometimes move out of their domain and mix up with men and women. Those who find themselves in the forest in their dreams are part of the victims of the night raiders.

Wandering spirits - These spirits wander about looking for people to possess.

Evil angels - These powers go about like normal human beings, only to disappear whenever their identity is about to be known. Just as there are good angels, there are also bad or evil angels. The good thing about good angels is that a single angel can destroy thousands of Satan's angels. For example, one angel of God destroyed 185,000 Assyrians in the Bible.

Power Against Dream Criminals

Satanic angels - These are fallen angels. They are wicked angels who double as men and angels and deal with human beings.

Wicked personalities - These wicked personalities carry out wicked assignments. Recently, a strange woman was caught in a posh area in Lagos, Nigeria. She was upturning people's dust bins in the neighbourhood searching for something. Once she realised that she could not find what she was looking for, she would turn the contents back to the dust bin. Then she would go to the next dust bin. Unknown to her, somebody was watching her from a distance.

The person watching her suddenly realised that she was excited whenever she found a used menstrual pad in a dust bin. The observer saw she put the pad in her handbag and resumed her search. The observer recognised that she was looking for nothing but used menstrual pads. She was gathering as many used pads as possible. No doubt, she was carrying out an evil assignment. It was clear that she wanted to use peoples' sanitary pads to do something against them.

Occult powers - Lodge members, Freemasons and other occult groups hold their meetings at night.

Spirit wives and spirit husbands - These forces go about at night raiding innocent men and women.

Ancestral strongmen - These spirits arrest people in the night.

Power Against Dream Criminals

Recruitment agents - These powers recruit or initiate men and women into all kinds of evil societies.

Spirits impersonating the dead - Some spirits impersonate dead people. It is because of these that there are reports of dead people who are seen in real life.

Satanic spies - These spies work like spiritual intelligence officers. Their task is to gather information concerning people which they take back to the Satanic kingdom.

Counterfeit angels - These forces pretend as if they are angels of God while they are not.

Dream manipulators - They manipulate people's dreams.

The Eater's of flesh and drinkers of blood - Their task is to destroy and cause all kinds of health problems.

Spirits from the second heavens - The second heaven is the place where darkness reigns. Spirits from that realm go about destroying peoples' lives.

Night caterers - They feed people with evil meals in their dreams at night.

The demon of pestilence - The Bible has stated that pestilence moves about in the night.

Local masquerades - They are part of the company of the evil night raiders.

Power Against Dream Criminals

Demon idols - These idols are sent to pursue and attack men and women.

Household pursuers - These powers operate within the household and attack members of the family.

Spirits of death and hell - These spirits also operate in the night. They are killer spirits.

Can you imagine what happens when these 24 powers decide to attack human beings? Unfortunately, there are people who are attacked by forces from more than 15 groups.

Now close your eyes and take this prayer point? *Every activity of satanic night raiders, be frustrated, in the name of Jesus.*

CHARACTERISTICS OF THE NIGHT RAIDERS

They are persistent - They have great determination and zeal. They are always at their duty posts. They avoid offending Satan, their task master is very cruel. They have compiled a list of all our weaknesses and use them as points of persistent attacks.

They are persuasive - They persuade people to carry out ungodly assignments. They push men and women to do what will make it easy for evil powers to attack them.

Power Against Dream Criminals

They are punctual and committed - They are always on time. If demons visit a particular person at 1.00 a.m. they will never be late. They do not miss their hour.

They are liars and deceivers - They show you all kinds of things in order to deceive you.

They are very productive - They always achieve maximum success. If these powers are not succeeding there will be no need to have deliverance ministers. Every night raider is a specialist. It knows how to do the right thing at the right time.

They are powerful in their own right - The Bible says: "When I was with you daily in the temple, ye stretched forth no hand against me but this is your hour and the power of darkness" (Luke 22:53). Here, Jesus admitted that powers of darkness have their own kind of power. However, although they are powerful, their own power is inferior to ours.

Today, a lot of people experience night visitations. Some are tired of these visitations but do not know what to do. Others keep the experience to themselves. These powers try to visit everyone. They do not want to give people breathing space. Their purpose is to kill, steal and destroy.

You may not be able to prevent evil powers from attempting to visit you, but you must not allow their weapons to prosper in your life. These powers visited Jesus but failed. Unfortunately, today, the weapons of the evil night raiders are prospering in

Power Against Dream Criminals

the lives of so many people. Very few people are victorious over these night raiders.

Some people are helpless whenever they are attacked by raiders at night. Some are so weak that they cannot call the name of Jesus when they are attacked. Some people would fight battles until they wake up in the morning. They become tired as if they had fought a real battle.

I do not know how many blows you have received from such night raiders. It is possible to experience victory at the end of a night raid only to wake up the next day with a swollen face. I am sure you know that there are some boxers who win in a boxing tournament only to be hospitalised for one week after the fight. That is why you must not joke with any encounter with night raiders. Therefore, I want you to take this prayer point.

Every satanic visitation at night assigned against my life, fall down and die, in the name of Jesus.

I have heard stories of people who go to bed hale and hearty only to experience a cold chill suddenly. Unless you know how to pray, the cold chill may continue for some time before it stops. You may then conclude that everything is over. You may not know they have planted something in your life. If you wake up the next day and rush to see a doctor, the doctor may prescribe some drugs for you but nothing will be able to take away the sickness because it is a spiritual attack.

Power Against Dream Criminals

There are those who are healthy only to, suddenly, receive an attack of paralysis all over their bodies. That is not an ordinary sickness. Others experience a swelling without knowing why. Sometimes some people observe that their heads become larger than usual. It is an evidence of an evil attack. Others are pressed down by some unseen forces when they are asleep. Some people would almost pass out because some unseen forces choked their throat. Others experience attacks from masquerades. Some are shot by uniformed soldiers in the dream.

If you have ever had a dream, in which you were shot by soldiers take this prayer point: *I fire back every satanic bullet, in the name of Jesus.*

A lot of people suffer from attacks of night raiders by receiving evil visitations from demon idols. Demon idols are short or small in stature. They are harsh and stone-faced. They go straight for their victims and attack them.

Sometimes when they attack, there is no physical evidence of their presence. It may be in form of a wind. Their victims would only feel a sharp pain in their bodies.

Recently, a lady shared a testimony with me. She was invited to a meeting and strangely the only vacant seat was given to her. She sat down not knowing that some powers had planned evil against her. She sat down not suspecting any foul play.

Power Against Dream Criminals

Suddenly, something was fired from the seat into her body. She was afraid. Fortunately for her, she heard the voice of the Holy Spirit "Don't let that arrow get to the region of your head." She promptly obeyed the instruction. What saved her is the fact that she was a prayer addict who always went about with her anointing oil. She stood up from her seat and rushed into the toilet, opened her bag, brought out the anointing oil and anointed her head. That was how God delivered her from that evil arrow. If she had not obeyed the voice of the Holy Spirit, she would have died on the chair and passed to eternity.

Victims of night raiders have all kinds of experiences. Some of them hear strange voices without seeing any human being. Others find themselves arraigned in a court in their dreams. Others dream and find themselves among a company of people in black uniform. If you do not pray about that kind of dream, you might be initiated forcefully into the demonic society.

Some of these night raiders are so effective that they do not have to touch their victims before planting evil objects in their lives. I wonder if there is anyone who has never had a visit from these night raiders at one time or the other.

If you have noticed that you are stagnant instead of breaking new grounds, then you can be sure that night raiders are at work.

If you have noticed that your dream life is a war front, night raiders are at work.

Power Against Dream Criminals

If you have noticed that you always have one funny dream or the other whenever you are about doing something that is very important, then you must be aware of the fact that night raiders are fighting against you.

If your being attacked in the dream makes you to experience automatic failure in real life, you do not need anyone to tell you that night raiders are carrying out some wicked activities in your life.

WHY NIGHT RAIDERS PROSPER

The power of God has not changed. It has never failed and will never fail. The problem is not with God but with us. You may ask: Why should night raiders prosper in the life of a child of God? The reasons are obvious.

Sin - Night raiders have legal rights over those who are living in sin, to trespass and attack them. So, if you are living in sin, you are exposing yourself to attacks from night raiders. If you have sex outside marriage, you are destroying yourself and throwing an invitation to night raiders.

Curses in place - Night raiders carry out their activities wherever they find unbroken curses in people's lives.

Evil covenants - Evil covenants are fertile ground for operation by evil night raiders.

Power Against Dream Criminals

Evil properties - Evil properties may include stolen goods, demonised objects which could be your earrings or your shoes, cursed art works and other materials. Such goods attract night raiders.

Lack of deliverance - Whenever there is incomplete deliverance or lack of deliverance in your life, evil powers will attack you.

Bad spiritual environment - If you happen to live in an environment that is spiritually contaminated, you are likely to experience evil visitations from night raiders. Or if you live in a place where sin abound, you will be open to attacks.

Backsliding - When you talk about backsliding, some people think about those who have turned their backs at God. That is not true. A backslider is anyone who fails to follow the Lord wholeheartedly. Those who refuse to obey the word of God, or allow sins in their lives, those who are crooked in their dealings with others, those who turn back to the devil, those who forget God and those who have left their first love and are now lukewarm.

If you deny Jesus as Peter did, look back like Lot's wife, or remain stagnant in your spiritual life, you are a backslider. You must settle your account with God today.

The only way you can be free from evil night raiders is to totally surrender your life unto God. If you allow evil night raiders to gain access into any department of your life, you will

Power Against Dream Criminals

be attacked. Get rid of everything that invites evil powers into your life today. Pray until you are free from every attack of night raiders.

6
JUDAS OF THE NIGHT

THE SPIRIT OF JUDAS AND THE SPIRIT OF THE NIGHT

There are certain elements that are identified with the night. An understanding of the characteristics of these elements would go a long way to make us understand certain spiritual realities. It is also important to understand what I have tagged the 'spirit of Judas.'

There is a mystery behind the spirit of Judas. By the time these two elements - the spirit of Judas and the spirit of the night join forces together they end up creating a dilemma.

Those who are well tutored in the art of spiritual warfare have learnt never to take anything for granted. Day to day events that take place in our lives may seem ordinary. But the truth is that before any event takes place in the physical realm, it has been designed and orchestrated in the spiritual realm. Therefore, we need the gift of discernment to properly interpret the going-ons around us.

When God opens our eyes, we shall come to the understanding of the facts that behind every physical action are spiritual force. These forces could be negative or positive. By the time you are through with this message you will see things in a different perspective and you will be armed with spiritual weapons to combat evil force that try to affect your life negatively.

Power Against Dream Criminals

It is my prayer that God would teach your fingers to fight and your hands to war. You need some preparations, however, in order to experience victory over the powers of Judas and of the night. Close your eyes as you take the following prayer points with spiritual aggression.

1. I release myself from the grip of the spirit of slumber, in the name of Jesus.

2. Every ladder of the enemy in my family, be roasted, in the name of Jesus.

3. I shake myself loose from every satanic entanglement, in the name of Jesus.

For the proper understanding of the term Judas of the night, we shall examine the scriptures.

> Matthew 26:31-35: Then saith Jesus unto them, All ye shall be offended because of me this night: for it is written, I will smite the shepherd, and the sheep of the flock shall be scattered abroad. [32]But after I am risen again, I will go before you into Galilee. [33]Peter answered and said unto him, Though all *men* shall be offended because of thee, *yet* will I never be offended. [34]Jesus said unto him, Verily I say unto thee, That this night, before the cock crow, thou shalt deny me thrice. [35]Peter said unto him, Though I should die with thee, yet will I not deny thee. Likewise also said all the disciples.

This is a very interesting story. Jesus addressed the disciples at a crucial time in the history of the church. The Lord has gained insight into the enemies grand-plan and the roles the

Power Against Dream Criminals

disciples were to play inadvertently. The disciples had no inkling whatsoever into what satan was up to.

Peter was over confident, he was so sure that he would never deny the Lord. Perhaps Peter was presumptuous instead of giving what the Lord was saying a second thought he was quick to say that he would never be offended. The Lord even helped him by predicting that Peter would deny him three times. At that point, Peter stated that he would rather die with his master than deny the Lord. One would have thought that the rest of the disciples would have learnt a lesson from Peter's brash statements. They did not. They echoed Peter's empty words. They all stated that they were ready to die with Jesus.

Let us read the story further.

> Matthew 26:36-56: Then cometh Jesus with them unto a place called Gethsemane, and saith unto the disciples, Sit ye here, while I go and pray yonder. [37]And he took with him Peter and the two sons of Zebedee, and began to be sorrowful and very heavy. [38]Then saith he unto them, My soul is exceeding sorrowful, even unto death: tarry ye here, and watch with me. [39]And he went a little farther, and fell on his face, and prayed, saying, O my Father, if it be possible, let this cup pass from me: nevertheless not as I will, but as thou *wilt*. [40]And he cometh unto the disciples, and findeth them asleep, and saith unto Peter, What, could ye not watch with me one hour? [41]Watch and pray, that ye enter not into temptation: the spirit indeed *is* willing, but the flesh *is* weak. [42]He went away again the second time, and prayed, saying, O my Father, if this cup may not pass away from me, except I drink it, thy will be

Power Against Dream Criminals

done. ⁴³And he came and found them asleep again: for their eyes were heavy. ⁴⁴And he left them, and went away again, and prayed the third time, saying the same words. ⁴⁵Then cometh he to his disciples, and saith unto them, Sleep on now, and take *your* rest: behold, the hour is at hand, and the Son of man is betrayed into the hands of sinners. ⁴⁶Rise, let us be going: behold, he is at hand that doth betray me. ⁴⁷And while he yet spake, lo, Judas, one of the twelve, came, and with him a great multitude with swords and staves, from the chief priests and elders of the people. ⁴⁸Now he that betrayed him gave them a sign, saying, Whomsoever I shall kiss, that same is he: hold him fast. ⁴⁹And forthwith he came to Jesus, and said, Hail, master; and kissed him. ⁵⁰And Jesus said unto him, Friend, wherefore art thou come? Then came they, and laid hands on Jesus, and took him. ⁵¹And, behold, one of them which were with Jesus stretched out *his* hand, and drew his sword, and struck a servant of the high priest's, and smote off his ear. ⁵²Then said Jesus unto him, Put up again thy sword into his place: for all they that take the sword shall perish with the sword. ⁵³Thinkest thou that I cannot now pray to my Father, and he shall presently give me more than twelve legions of angels? ⁵⁴But how then shall the scriptures be fulfilled, that thus it must be? ⁵⁵In that same hour said Jesus to the multitudes, Are ye come out as against a thief with swords and staves for to take me? I sat daily with you teaching in the temple, and ye laid no hold on me. ⁵⁶But all this was done, that the scriptures of the prophets might be fulfilled. Then all the disciples forsook him, and fled.

We have lots of messages to learn from this passage as regards the practical nitty-gritty of spiritual warfare.

Power Against Dream Criminals

This passage throws so much light on the subject you are considering "Judas of the Night".

THE SPIRIT OF JUDAS

Two words stand out "Judas and Night". Let us focus our attention on Judas for now.

Names are very significant. They tell us so much about spiritual and physical realities. Most of the names and event we come across in the Old Testament have relevance in the New Testament. In fact, the New Testament centres on the out working of Old Testament themes and events.

Whenever reference is made in the Bible to certain names, we will do well to check up on their meanings. Judas happens to be a good name. It is a derivative form of the name Jude which means "praised". Here the name suggests being praised or receiving commendation. In this regard, good as the name sounds, there is an ugly spirit behind it.

For the purpose of proper analysis and instructive study, let us examine the characteristics of the spirit of Judas. I counsel you to be sincere with yourself and accept the truth. Should you discover these traits in your life, that is, if the spirit of Judas is working in your life, you owe yourself a duty of praying until every trait is consumed by the fire of the Holy Ghost.

Power Against Dream Criminals

THE CHARACTERISTICS OF THE SPIRIT OF JUDAS

☞ *It is the spirit of the thief*

This is a very stubborn spirit. According to Bible records, Judas was a thief, although he was close to Jesus, yet he stole money from the offering bag. This is common today in many churches.

Moreover, Judas also allowed the spirit of theft to push him to receive money in exchange for the betrayal of His master. So do many people today follow Judas' foot-steps. They accept all forms of gratification in order to put their friends or those to whom they had pledged loyalty into trouble.

☞ *It is the spirit of hypocrisy*

This is the spirit of a perfect pretender. We have such people today. They have mastered the art of ambivalence. They are double faced. They share something in common with the Chameleon, you can never know where they belong.

☞ *A dual personality*

A lot of people belong to this category, such people are smart actors. They can play any part assigned to them. That is the spirit of Judas.

☞ *The ability to operate as an unfriendly friend*

Unfriendly friends abound today. They act like friends but they are enemies. Such people may claim that they are your

Power Against Dream Criminals

friends but they will go ahead and do things that are against your interest.

☞ *The spirit of the satanic kiss*

Such a kiss is evil to the core. It is poisonous.

☞ *It is the spirit of deception*

This spirit is very deceptive. Deception is rife in the church today. Many people play the game of deception without being detected.

☞ *The spirit of betrayal*

A lot of people are busy betraying their masters like Judas. This is common in these last days.

☞ *The spirit of wickedness*

Those who are possessed by the spirit of Judas go into acts of wickedness without batting an eye lid. How can anyone decide to sell someone like the Lord Jesus Christ? That is the spirit of Judas for you.

☞ *The spirit that questions the word of God*

People who belong to this category pick holes in the word of God and go about looking for personal interpretations that would suit their own whims and caprices. Judas had an eye on political power. He wanted Jesus to take over the government of the day, so that he would become a governor. However, this did not work out according to his expectation.

Power Against Dream Criminals

☞ *The spirit of suicide*

It can also be referred to as the spirit of death. Judas ended his life in the school of suicide. This spirit is still working in the lives of many people today.

The devil would want you to believe that these characteristics are no longer in operation today. Do not be hooked on the devil's lies. These things are still happening today.

A strange event occurred a few years ago. It was a very interesting event. A police officer who happened to be a member of the Mountain of Fire and Miracles Ministries was busy performing his official duties when two people dragged themselves to the station.

A man and a woman came to lodge a strange complaint. According to the woman's claims, the man was indebted to her to the tune of two hundred and Fifty Thousand naira (₦250,000:00). According to the woman, the amount was collected for a deal that was never performed by the man.

You wonder what the deal was all about? The police officer was told that the man was paid the money, simply because he wanted him to make use of fetish powers to kill the woman's husband. It was then it became clear that the elderly man who was accused to breach of contract was a fetish priest otherwise called herbalist in Nigerian English. The fetish priest now opened up and narrated his own side of the story.

Power Against Dream Criminals

"Police officer, let me tell you the truth. Madam actually paid me for terminating the life of her husband. As usual, I started with some good results. Initially my efforts yielded good results."

He continued,

"All of a sudden, things got out of hand. Some strange powers took madam's husband to a realm where my fetish power could no longer have any effect on him. To be honest, I've tried my best but this has proved to be a stubborn case. I don't know why I just couldn't succeed. Madam's husband seems to be enjoying the protection of some superior powers."

Do you know what, we later discovered, the man whom the evil messenger had hired to kill happened to be a member of our church? The situation became problematic for the fetish priest the moment the woman's husband found his way to the Mountain of Fire and Miracles.

This is a classical example of the operation of the spirit of Judas. A woman decided to pay such a large sum of money in order to kill her husband. You can imagine how many husbands have died through the sinister or diabolical actions of their wives. The best thing that can happen to you is to get to a point where you begin to pray against the spirit of Judas that is hiring satanic priests or fetish priests for your sake.

Power Against Dream Criminals

THE SPIRIT OF THE NIGHT

I am sure at this point that you are quite familiar with the workings of the spirit of Judas. Let us now examine the spirit of the night. Although Judas was the culprit that betrayed Jesus, yet, there is a mystery attached to the night according to the thirty-first verse of our text: "Then saith Jesus unto them, all ye shall be offended because of me this night".

There are certain points to note about the night whenever you come across the use of words in the scriptures. Let us examine the salient features of the night, which bother on spiritual warfare.

☞ *Darkness*

The first and the most important characteristics of the night is darkness. Significantly, God was the first person to call the night darkness. This is recorded in the scriptures.

> Genesis 1:5: And God called the light Day, and the darkness he called Night. And the evening and the morning were the first day.

The mystery of darkness needs to be understood here. We need to understand how God distinguishes the night from the day. Again this is stated very clearly in the scriptures.

> Genesis 1:14-18: And God said, Let there be lights in the firmament of the heaven to divide the day from the night; and let them be for signs, and for seasons, and for days, and years: [15]And let them be for lights in the firmament of the heaven to

Power Against Dream Criminals

give light upon the earth: and it was so. [16]And God made two great lights; the greater light to rule the day, and the lesser light to rule the night: *he made* the stars also, [17]And God set them in the firmament of the heaven to give light upon the earth, [18]And to rule over the day and over the night, and to divide the light from the darkness: and God saw that *it was* good.

God used heavenly bodies to separate the day from the night. God established two great lights; the sun to rule the day and the moon to rule the night. You can only understand this when you read the psalms.

Psalm 121:6: The sun shall not smite thee by day, nor the moon by night.

Thus you would understand the fact that what is written in the book of Genesis concerning the sun and the moon is deeper than any of us can imagine. This is the import of the mystery of darkness.

The sun rules day while the moon rules the night, therefore, if you pray saying the sun shall not smite me by day nor the moon by night, you are handling a great prayer point. Why don't you close your eyes and take this powerful prayer point;

The moon shall not oppose my day, in the name of Jesus.

Did you take that prayer point? Please do.

The moon appears gentle and harmless but it smites those who undermine its powers.

Power Against Dream Criminals

You need to pray against the angles of the night and day that are working for the devil. If you allow the powers of the night to strike you, you may suffer untold physical and spiritual havoc.

Generally darkness is characterised by the absence of light and knowledge, as well as being partially blind. Without doubt, many are passing through gruelling darkness. At this point, if you are one of such you must deliver yourself from the power of the night.

☞ *The night commences as the sun sets*

Immediately the sun begins to set, the mystery of the night begins. The enemy is busy making the suns of many men and women to set abruptly. The devil does this when the sun of the lives of many people is at the fullest strength.

☞ The night is generally considered unsuitable for labour.

Jesus said, "I must work the works of him that sent me while it is day; the night cometh when no man can work" (John 9:4).

The enemy has converted the days of many to night.

☞ *The night is normally designed for rest.*

The enemy has forced many to retire from God's best.

☞ *Night is wearisome to the afflicted*

Those who are sickly are generally afraid of night time.

Power Against Dream Criminals

☞ *The night is favourable to the purpose of the wicked*

Whenever the wicked wants to operate they opt for the cover of the night. Wild beasts for example go in search of their prey in the night.

That is why in Bible days, shepherds generally keep watch over their flocks in the night. They do this in order to keep them safe from wicked predators.

Thieves operate mostly at night. These facts go a long way to prove that the night is favourable to the operations of the wicked.

☞ *The Bible identifies the night as a period of serious calamity*

It is a period of spiritual desertion. Jesus passed through that period. It was so serious that He cried out, "My Lord, My God, why has Thou forsaken me?"

☞ *The night also refers to the period of death*

The moment a man stops breathing, he can no longer do any work. That is why Jesus said the night cometh when no man can work.

I want you to close this book for a while as you take these three life changing prayer points.

1. The enemy shall not convert my day to night, in the name of Jesus.

Power Against Dream Criminals

2. What the enemy has stolen from me at night, I posses my possession, in the name of Jesus.

3. I dismantle every satanic transfer of my goodness, in the name of Jesus.

PRE-EMPTIVE ATTACK- WATCH AND PRAY

No army attacks another army without doing proper home work. Preparations are generally made concerning how to achieve victory within the shortest possible time and with the smallest casualty rate. The leader of a wise army will examine the human and material resources at his disposal. This is made abundantly clear in the scriptures.

> Luke 14:31-32: Or what king, going to make war against another king, sitteth not down first, and consulteth whether he be able with ten thousand to meet him that cometh against him with twenty thousand? ³²Or else, while the other is yet a great way off, he sendeth an ambassage, and desireth conditions of peace.

Wars are not won by the strength of any army. Much depends on the commander. Sometimes we have had instances of weak armies gaining victory over strong ones.

Do you know what weaker nations often do? They spring surprises by attacking stronger nations at an unexpected hour.

Power Against Dream Criminals

This happened in 1967 during the Egypt-Israel war. The Arabs and Russians were solidly behind Egypt. The ratio of the war tanks and other weapons which Egypt had was ten to one, placing Egypt at an advantage knowing that she would suffer terrible losses. Israel adopted an intelligent warfare strategy. They launched an offensive attack on Egypt at an unexpected hour. Before Egypt could get ready for warfare or hostilities, the battle had already ended.

This is called the 'Pre-emptive Strategy' in military palance.

This strategy was adopted by satan against the nation of Israel according to Numbers 22:24, Moab discovered that Israel was too powerful to contend with, they taught of a winning strategy. They had hired Balaam and he had failed woefully. They used an unusual method. They sent their girls to the camp of the Israelites. They mandated these agents to seduce Israel. What they could not do through warfare they achieved through seduction.

This is an example of pre-emptive attack. Before Israel could gather itself together, the enemy nation launched an attack. Since God was angry with the children of Israel, the edge of protection and the mantle of victory, fell off.

ATTACK OF THE SPIRIT OF THE NIGHT
- *The spirit of slumber*

Satan is not a fool. He is aware of the fact that he fights the church from where victory is impossible. He therefore tries to launch an attack by introducing a strategy that would weaken the position of God's people.

God does not want any of His children to be a victim of satanic attacks. Jesus has not kept us in the dark. Just like He told the disciples, He wants us to be aware of the fact that the night of satanic attack is imminent. Do not be caught unawares; the devil is planing another invasion.

Beloved, a night, a very dark one, a night of offence is near. A night of fierce trials and persecution is at hand. Do not be deceived, beloved, a night of backsliding and denial is near. These and other things were predicted by Jesus during His earthly ministry.

However, He taught them how to deal with such sudden satanic attacks. He told them, specially, to watch and pray. This is also what we must do if we want to experience victory over the powers of the night.

The disciples of Jesus failed to carry out the instruction given to them by Jesus and made themselves vulnerable to satanic attacks.

Power Against Dream Criminals

They failed to use the weapon of prayer. And before they could gather themselves together, the devil lunched an offensive against them. He shot the arrow of slumber into their camp. Instead of watching in prayer, they slumbered and slept. The devil has continued to use this weapon to cage many lives.

Sleep is a deadly satanic weapon. If you have allowed sleep to steal or kill your prayer life, you are already in the enemies' cage. You are under the attack of the spirit of the night. This is not the time when Christian believers should sleep. The time for sleep and rest, still lies ahead of us. This is stated clearly in the scriptures.

> Hebrews 4:9: There remaineth therefore a rest to the people of God.

Satan knew that if the disciples kept awake and continued to pray aggressively, they would win the battle and spoil his plan for the hour of temptation.

Thus, he employed the strategy that swept them off their feet. They slept, when they were supposed to be watching. Thus, they did not know when disaster was lurking around them. Thus they were scattered by the enemy. But how could those who had come a long way with Christ become scattered in one day? That is the power of slumber. Instead of watching with Christ for one more hour, they slept.

Let me make these important statements. In every age, before satan strikes, he normally sends the spirit of slumber as a forerunner. He does this to get rid of those who are supposed

Power Against Dream Criminals

to be keeping awake to watch against impending attacks. Therefore, you must watch against signals which reminds you of the fact that the spirit of slumber has made the territory of your life a landing strip.

If you now sleep during your devotional hour, you have a great problem on hand. It is even worse, if you find yourself sleeping during the time of worship.

The devil knows that if he uses the weapon of sleep, he will have very little difficulty in taking you captive, that is why he uses that weapon all the time.

Sleep or slumber is dangerous. It portends lots of danger. Sleep is ominous. In every age, spiritual disaster has always followed moments of spiritual slumber.

Examine biblical history and you will discover that moments of slumber lead to times of darkness.

Revival comes when people watch and pray. Slumber on the other hand invites disaster. I pity those who sleep when they are supposed to be praying. Anyone who falls into that category is caged. Such a person has been overtaken by the flesh. We do not need a prophet to tell such a fellow that disaster is at hand.

Slumber or sleep is the forerunner of tragedy.

Right now I want you to close your eyes and deal with the spirit of slumber once and for all.

Power Against Dream Criminals

Put the totality of your strength into these prayer points.

1. I bind every spirit of slumber, it shall not cage my life, in the name of Jesus.

2. My angel of blessing shall not find me sleeping, in the name of Jesus.

CONFLICT BETWEEN THE SPIRIT AND THE FLESH

Jesus has surveyed the entire gamut of the power of the night and given us a panacea for dealing with it. He struck at the root of the problem of man when He said the spirit indeed is willing but the flesh is weak. The Lord wants us to come to the realisation of the fact that at the root of man's problem lies the conflict between the spirit and the flesh. It is true that your spirit wants to pray but the flesh is weak. When the spirit wants to pull in one direction, the flesh pulls towards the opposite direction. In other words, there are two forces at work. These actions and reactions produce negative results.

We have therefore become the battle ground of two opposing forces; the spirit and the flesh. You may ask, why are these two forces fighting each other? It is simply because you hold the key to the outcome of what happens in the night.

Unfortunately, in the case of the disciples, the flesh gained an upper hand and won. The devil won and the disciples lost out.

Power Against Dream Criminals

No wonder, they fled in the morning. Why? They failed in the night. Darkness invaded their territory and they became afraid. Sleep, the forerunner of the real battle won the first round of the duel, then the Judas of the night came to conclude the conquest.

The members of the army of Judas came with all their fury against the camp of the disciples. I am sure you know the rest of the story.

Trouble, dispersion, fear and backsliding were the negative results of not being prepared for the attack by the spirit of the night.

I plead with you to set a watch over your life. What do you do when the spirit of God prevails on you, by instructing you to pray? Do you give excuses, promising to pray at a more convenient time? If you fail to heed the voice of the Holy Spirit you are opening the door of your life for the spirit of Judas to come in.

I wonder how a Christian who knows that this is the hour of battle should decide to sleep throughout the night. If you refuse to pray after persistent nudging by the Holy Spirit, you may be given over to a reprobate prayer-less life.

A time may come when you will become indifferent to prayer. Jesus told the disciples to watch; they did not. At a point He told them "sleep on now" that was a dangerous moment in their lives. If you enter into that kind of sleep

Power Against Dream Criminals

realm, you will pay dearly for it. The enemy will attack you and you will no longer be able to sleep. Watch it!

The spirit of slumber is the ruling spirit in these last days. It has been released by the devil to destroy several lives.

Do you know that many of the important spiritual battles are won after midnight? There is nothing as powerful as midnight prayer. Life's greatest battles are often fought after mid-night. Here in Africa, terrible demonic meetings are held between the hours of twelve and three in the night. That is why God wakes up several people to pray during those hours.

Unfortunately many have continued to silence the voice of God because they prefer sleeping to praying.

Under the influence of the power of slumber the disciples found it difficult to obey the commandments of Jesus. They could not watch and pray. This is what happens when you allow the flesh to gain the upper hand. You will not be able to obey God. You generally hear two voices. The flesh will tell you sleep, while the Lord will warn you to pray, this is not your hour of rest.

The problem here is that it is easier to listen to the voice of the flesh than to obey the voice of the Holy Spirit. This explains why spiritual things have become extremely burdensome for many people today. For the disciple, that night was the beginning of the dispensation of the flesh. During that

Power Against Dream Criminals

disposition the spirit suffered untold damage. The flesh reigned without a rival.

Unfortunately, a lot of people are living in that dispensation. This is the sleeping season for many so-called Christians. We are living in a dangerous era. I counsel you to snatch your self from the powers of the night. If you fail to do so, the brigade of Judas will invade your life.

If you fail to wake up and begin a life changing revival, the spirit of Judas will suffocate your spiritual life.

If you allow the noise of snoring to go on at the altar of your life instead of the voice of prayer, the brigade of Judas will capture every department of your life.

Any believer who wants to be serious with God must get ready to attack the spirit of slumber.

You must run yourself through a session of a personal spiritual checkup.

Do you generally allow the spirit of the flesh to rule your life? Are you fond of giving in to the spirit of slumber? Do you find it easier to please the flesh than to please the Holy Spirit? Do you cherish every opportunity to go into slumber and complain whenever you are told to engage in spiritual exercises like praying and fasting?

Examine yourself.

Power Against Dream Criminals

God is aware of the fact that of all strategies used by the devil, the spirit of slumber has proved to be most effective. That is why He is warning us today.

The spirit of slumber is the devil of this generation. The spirit of Judas is getting ready to destroy once again. The armies of the night are getting ready to invade the lives of multitudes. The only antidote centres on being re-awakened and being put on fire. The moment you begin to watch and pray, you would begin to subdue the flesh. Church workers, couples and brethren who keep vigil in the night and pray instead of sleeping will always experience resounding victory.

This message is God's word and may land you in trouble. I counsel you to go on your knees and repent of every way you have been giving heed to spiritual slumber. Ask God to revive your prayer life.

NEXT STAGE - EVIL DREAMS

I want you to take cognizant of the fact that anything can happen after you have decided to allow the spirit of slumber to dominate your life. The devil will then go on to use another wicked weapon; the weapon of evil dreams.

Victims of this kind of satanic attack will begin to have all kinds of useless and frightening dreams. The moment you enter the realm of the night and the armies of Judas have

Power Against Dream Criminals

captured your life, then your dream life will become a battle field.

The devil will use the following categories of dreams to attack you.

When you dream of being abandoned. It is an indication of the fact that the devil wants you to loose your friends. Loss of friend and favour is inevitable.

When you dream and see yourself lonely and deserted you have lots of trouble on your hand.

If you dream about playing cards or games, you are going through moments of satanic manipulation.

If you always have contact with your ancestors in your dreams, sickness and spiritual attacks are on the prowl.

If you dream of engaging in physical combat with armed men, you are under the attack of the army of Judas.

If you see demonic barbers trying to give you an air cut in your dreams, evil powers are trying to remove your glory.

If you fight with a bat in your dream, it is an implication of the fact that the devil is trying to use pretenders and hypocrisies against you.

If you find yourself loosing blood in the dream, the enemy is trying to make you loose your virtue.

Power Against Dream Criminals

If you find handcuffs on your hands or if you find yourself putting on earrings as a man or a woman in your dream, it shows that the enemy is trying to put you under bondage.

If you dream about crabs, the enemy is trying to introduce disorderliness into your life.

If you see dead parents or relatives in your dreams, then the spirit of the death has been programmed against you.

If the devil has harassed you with these and other kinds of dreams, you can put the satanic machine out of use.

STRATEGIES FOR PREVENTING BAD DREAMS

Let me give you the strategy for preventing bad dreams. You can also use this strategy to combat the problem of slumber.

☞ *Self examination*

Examine yourself, make sure that you are not living in any known sin. Sin will always create room for the devil. You must repent and renounce sin like fornication, lying, adultery, anger etc. If you live a sinful life you will always have bad dreams.

☞ *Always fortify your inner man with the word of God*

Power Against Dream Criminals

Learn at least two memory verses per week. The strength of your spirit man lies in the word of God.

- *Engage yourself in meaningful praise worship before going to bed at night*
- *Pray aggressive prayers before you go to bed*

In case you do not know what prayer points to use, you can get yourself copies of the following prayer manuals. Pray your way to break through, Prayer Rain, Violent Prayers to Disgrace Stubborn Problems.

- *Never go to bed angry or in a fighting mood*

To sleep when you are depressed or sad is to invite bad dreams.

- *Avoid reading dirty books, watching dirty films engaging in idle chatter and cracking dirty jokes before going to bed*
- *Worry and anxiety must not be allowed ever to reign in your life*
- *Pray that God's angels and His fire should surround your dwelling place before you sleep*
- *Anoint your room periodically*

This will go a long way in keeping the edge of protection intact.

- *Bind the activities of the spirit of slumber*

Power Against Dream Criminals

PRAYER POINTS

1. I declare that it is the word of God concerning my life that is settled in heaven, no evil dream of my life is settled in heaven. I bind myself to the blood of Jesus. I bind myself to positive dreams. I loose myself from negative dreams. Every dream, vision, prophecy, prediction that did not originate from the Holy Spirit, I render you null and void, in the name of Jesus.

2. I uproot and destroy every tree that my heavenly Father has not planted, in the name of Jesus.

3. Every spiritual bullet and arrow fired at me shall not prosper, in the name of Jesus.

4. From today, I insulate my life from every satanic influence, in the name of Jesus.

5. O Lord, let Your heavenly hosts and warriors take over my battle.

6. Lord of hosts, fight for me.

7. I resist every power of darkness, in the name of Jesus.

8. Any power trying to manipulate my life through dreams, get out of my ways, in the name of Jesus.

9. I reject every spirit of slumber, in the name of Jesus.

10. I claim victory over every satanic attack, in the name of Jesus.

Power Against Dream Criminals

11. Every defeat of the night, be converted to victory now, in the name of Jesus.

12. I refuse to be a prisoner in the cage of the enemy, in the name of Jesus.

13. O Lord, whatsoever will make me deaf to Your voice, take it out of my life, in the name of Jesus.

14. You wicked spirits and principalities present over the atmosphere of this nation, I destroy you in the name of Jesus.

15. Every satanic gathering in the heavenly against this nation, I scatter your counsel, it shall not stand, in the name of Jesus.

16. You satanic gathering of evil powers, plotting against this nation, I disperse you, your counsel shall not stand, your association shall not prosper, in the name of Jesus.

17. I speak evil against satanic gatherings, in the name of Jesus.

18. We speak against every spell and every covenant speaking against our land, in the name of Jesus.

19. I silence the satanic storms and reject them, and I crown Jesus King of kings, Lord of lords this day and forever in my country and beyond, in the name of Jesus.

7
VICTORY OVER SATANIC DREAMS

Power Against Dream Criminals

INTRODUCTION

Dreaming is a natural way in which the spirit world breaks out into our lives.

Dreams can be described as the dark speech of the spirit. Dreams are means of revelation. Unfortunately, modern men and women have chosen to either ignore dreams altogether or to fear that an interest in them is lack of civilization. The fact is that if we would listen, dreams can help us find increased spiritual victory and help.

Once we have the revelation that dreams can be a key to unlocking the door to the spirit world, we can take some vital steps.

First, we can specifically pray inviting God to inform us through our dreams.

Secondly, we should declare war when dreams are used against us.

Third, we should learn how to interpret dreams. The best way to discover the meaning of dreams is to ask the Holy Spirit.

It is worthy of note that God promised that He would speak to His people by dreams in the last days. Acts 2:17:

> And it shall come to pass in the last days, saith God, I will pour out of my Spirit upon all flesh: and your sons and your daughters shall prophesy, and your young men shall see visions, and your old men shall dream dreams.

Power Against Dream Criminals

Therefore, our dreams need to be studied and analyzed with a view to decoding their messages.

I want you to speak to the Lord now. Ask the Lord to make this day a special moment in your life. Tell Him to make this day a day you will never forget.

I have a somewhat difficult task at hand. But I know that the Lord will help me. I want you to be very attentive. I am sharing a life-changing truth with you today.

The message contained in this book is similar to a booklet I titled: Breaking Witchcraft Curses.

By the grace of God, we are looking at an important topic which, I believe, will lead to your total deliverance. The problems of most people can be traced to our subject of consideration. I am, therefore, speaking to you on: "Victory Over Satanic Dreams".

You have to read carefully and pay attention to the entire content of this booklet. Do not allow sleep or any distractions to rob you of the blessings of this booklet. The enemy of your soul will try and prevent you from reading this book with full concentration.

I know that the devil does not want you to experience victory over satanic dreams. But do not worry, the devil has been defeated for you.

Power Against Dream Criminals

SATANIC STRATEGIES

There is no other passage to turn to for a proper understanding of victory over satanic dreams than Matthew 13:25:

> But while men slept, his enemy came and sowed ...

A dream is a natural way in which the spiritual world breaks into our lives. Dreams can be keys to unlocking the door to the inner world.

Dreams have been referred to as the speech of the spirit. Unfortunately modern Christians have tended to either ignore dreams altogether or take them as playthings.

Every normal person is supposed to sleep. God in His own wisdom has designed this for man. Everything which God has designed for man is for a good purpose. But the problem is that the enemy goes into every good thing and corrupts it. The devil turns anything that should be a friend of man into an enemy.

Dreams play an active role in the lives of men and women. Unfortunately, the problems in the lives of most people start with instances of satanic dreams.

People face two types of danger.

One, a lot of people are so deep in spiritual sleep that they never remember what they dreamt about when they wake up. This is the twin danger; when somebody dreams and forgets everything, he stands the danger of missing an important

Power Against Dream Criminals

message or ministration from God if He was the One speaking through the dream.

Two, if the enemy is carrying out an evil activity and you forget the dream, you also face the danger of remaining under bondage. If you are fond of forgetting dreams on a regular basis, you have a very serious problem.

I remember the case of a sister who came to the church during the time we were having a seventy-day fasting and prayer session. We had a session tagged: "Know the Secrets." She went to the Lord and requested to know certain secrets.

As she was praying, God opened her eyes and she found herself before a great king who told her,

"Be careful about that church you are attending; I have only allowed you to go there because I know that you will never become a genuine member of the church."

Then she woke up. She came to me for counseling and told me about the dream. I told her,

"You have a strange king ruling over your life. Jesus is the only true King. You have a demonic king to dethrone in your life. You must dethrone that king and lift Jesus up."

She started praying, saying; "You strange king, be dethroned, in the mighty name of the Lord Jesus Christ." She was not fully aware of the problem she was bringing upon herself. The same

Power Against Dream Criminals

night she prayed, she found herself before the throne of that same king. The king was angry. He confronted her and said,

"What kind of nonsense is this? I know how to deal with you. I will remove your spiritual memory so that whatever you see or hear in a dream will never be remembered."

Since that day, the sister just sleeps and wakes without remembering any dream she had. As a result of her spiritual level, the devil kept on doing great havoc against her life without her knowledge. This sister eventually declared war against her oppressors and dethroned the foreign king. There is a double danger here. You need to pray against this type of problem.

DEMONIC ATTACKS

Sometimes, people experience the manifestations of what evil powers have done in the dream.

Most of the time, what happens in the realm of the dream happens in the physical as well. Another sister dreamt about somebody who was defecating on her head. She was worried. Unfortunately, she belonged to a fellowship where spiritual warfare is not taught. Since that day, her husband began to hate her. That marked the beginning of the ruin of her marriage.

Occasionally, satanic agents force people to eat in the dream. Problems often start with such strange dreams. The Bible says:

Power Against Dream Criminals

My people are destroyed for lack of knowledge (Hosea 4:6).

Many people have suffered terribly as a result of ignorance of what the devil does in dreams. Many people have fallen prey to the enemies through dreams. Many have been made to believe lies and errors through satanic dreams. The enemy has used dreams to confuse a lot of people in their marital, business, financial and spiritual matters.

TYPES OF DREAMS

A dream may come in the form of an activity which the dreamer is involved in. Apart from being an activity, a dream may come as an event. For example, the dreamer may find himself sitting down and watching the television.

Sometimes a dream could be centered on something which has occurred or something which is about to occur. The dream may also be a message to a particular person. Some people also dream strange dreams inside a dream. Of course, that is strange. Such people need prayer.

A dream sometimes comes as an attack on the dreamer. Some forces may start fighting against you in a dream. Whichever is your dream, the spirit world is trying to have an impact on your life.

SOURCES OF DREAMS

Therefore, dreams are generally a film of occurrences in the spiritual realm. Before we dig deep into the revelation concerning dreams, we want to take an incisive look into the sources of dreams. Where do dreams come from?

Dreams may come from God. This is demonstrated in Joseph's life.

> Now Israel loved Joseph more than all his children, because he was the son of his old age: and he made him a coat of many colours. And when his brethren saw that their father loved him more than all his brethren, they hated him, and could not speak peaceably unto him. And Joseph dreamed a dream, and he told it to his brethren: and they hated him yet the more. And he said unto them, Hear, I pray you, this dream which I have dreamed: For, behold, we were binding sheaves in the field, and, lo, my sheaf arose, and also stood upright; and, behold, your sheaves stood round about, and made obeisance to my sheaf (Genesis 37:3-7).

This account reveals that God revealed Joseph's life story to him in a dream.

The fact that God speaks to people through dreams is clearly enunciated in Numbers 12:6.

> And He said, Hear now My words: If there be a prophet among you, I the Lord will make Myself known unto him in a vision, and will speak unto him in a DREAM.

Power Against Dream Criminals

Another popular passage in the Bible further clarifies this point:

> And it shall come to pass afterwards, that I will pour out My Spirit upon all flesh, and your sons and your daughters shall prophesy, your old men shall DREAM DREAMS, your young men shall see visions (Joel 2:28).

This same verse was also quoted in Acts 2:17.

The Bible says:

> The prophet that hath a dream, let him tell a dream; and he that hath My word, let him speak My word faithfully. What is the chaff to the wheat? saith the LORD? (Jeremiah 23:28).

This passage shows us that a God-appointed prophet could have dreams. You might say that this is an old testament passage. But what will you say when you read a New Testament passage?

> And being warned of God in a DREAM that they should not return to Herod, they departed into their own country another way. And when they were departed, behold, the angel of the Lord appeareth to Joseph in a DREAM, saying, 'Arise, and take the young child and his mother, and flee into Egypt, and be thou there until I bring you word: for Herod will seek the young child to destroy him'. When he arose, he took the young child and his mother by night, and departed into Egypt (Matthew 2:12-14).

So, how did God speak to Joseph? God spoke to him through a dream. God speaks to people in dreams in order to instruct them concerning what to do. God also speaks to people in dreams in order to warn them. Let us look at Job 33:14-16:

> For God speaketh once, yea twice, yet we perceiveth it not. In a dream, in a vision of the night, when deep sleep falleth upon men, in slumberings upon the bed; then He openeth the ears of men, and sealeth their instruction.

God speaks to people in their dreams. Sometimes, people are too noisy. God, therefore, chooses to speak to them through dreams. Many people have formed the habit of tuning to local and foreign radio stations immediately they wake up in the morning.

So, when they go to work they also face the "noise" of traffic jam. Immediately they get to their office, they are bombarded with the noise of idle talk. When they close from work and they are on their way home, it is noise again. As soon as they get home, it is the noise of T.V.. So, the only time they experience any form of quietness at all is in the night when they are sleeping. That is the only time God can gain their attention if He wants to speak to them.

THE PURPOSE OF DREAMS

God can warn of an impending danger through a dream like He did to Joseph, the earthly father of Jesus.

Power Against Dream Criminals

He can also show you the blue-print for your life like He did to Joseph. God can also use a dream to rebuke a person. If the person complies with God's word, there will be grace and mercy.

God can also use dreams to reveal the plan of your life to you like He did in the case of Solomon.

> In Gibeon, the Lord appeared to Solomon in a dream by night: and God said, Ask what I shall give thee: And God said unto him, Because thou has asked this thing, and hast not asked for thyself long life; neither hast asked riches for thyself, nor hast asked the life of thine enemies; but has asked for thyself understanding to discern judgement: . . . And if thou wilt walk in My ways, to keep My statutes and My commandments, as thy father David did walk, then I will lengthen thy days. And Solomon awoke: and, behold, it was a dream . . . (1 Kings 3:5,11-15).

God can use dreams to encourage a person like He used it to encourage, direct, instruct and make covenants with Bible characters. There are many examples in the Bible.

Pharaoh dreamt about impending famine. The wise men who visited and gave gifts to Jesus when He was born were also directed through a dream.

Paul had a dream in which he was told: "Come over to Macedonia and help us." Pilate's wife also had a dream which made her to warn her husband to wash his hands clean from unlawful persecution of Jesus.

Power Against Dream Criminals

All these are practical examples.

Has God given you any dream about your life? Pray until it comes to pass. Remember, God does not give bad dreams to His Children. He only gives good dreams. The Bible says:

> For I know the thoughts that I think toward you, saith the Lord, thoughts of peace, and not of evil, to give you an expected end (Jeremiah 29:11).

Every God-given dream is for your good. If God has warned you through a dream to take an important or urgent step in your life, you must obey promptly. Please do so.

In conclusion, divine dreams can be divided into four kinds

- dreams of instruction or teaching
- dreams of the prophetic nature
- dreams of warning
- dreams of encouragement.

MENTAL DREAMS

Dreams also come from man. People dream about what they are pre-occupied with in their day-to-day activities:

> For a dream cometh through the multitude of business; and a fool's voice is known by multitude of words (Ecclesiastes 5:3).

Again the Bible says:

Power Against Dream Criminals

> For in the multitude of dreams and many words there are also divers vanities: but fear thou God (Ecclesiastes 5:7).

When a dream comes from man, God has nothing to do with it. Neither is the devil behind dreams which emanate from the mind of man. This is made very clear in the Scriptures:

> It shall even be as when an hungry man dreameth, and, behold, he eateth; but he awaketh, and his soul is empty: or as when a thirsty man dreameth, and, behold, he drinketh; but he awaketh, and, behold, he is faint, and his soul hath appetite ... (Isaiah 29:8).

You only dream about what occupies your mind throughout the day. When you fill a glass with water, a little tilt will spill some water.

If your heart is brimful with a particular thought, such thoughts will be replayed in your dreams.

Those who have given themselves to fornication and all forms of immorality, will dream about it.

Sad people will always dream about tragedy.

If you read a bad book before going to bed, you are likely to see horrible pictures of what you read in your dream.

If you read an occultic book, you will dream of weird and occultic things.

If you watch a terrible and corrupting television programme, you will see the same things in your dream.

Power Against Dream Criminals

INFLUENCE

If you are a believer who is fond of counting his woes, tragedies and misfortunes, you will do the same in your dreams.

If your dreams are completely taken over by worldly things and you are always dreaming of dancing at parties, you need to repent, your dreams are reflections of your state of mind.

Fleshly or carnal dreams can be so deceptive, especially when you have not crucified your flesh. To a large extent, if you are filthy, you will have filthy dreams.

If you are holy, you will have heavenly and God-honouring dreams.

Confused people have confusing and senseless dreams.

Demonic people have demonic dreams.

Sick people generally dream about sickness. There is a fitting example in the Book of Job:

> Now a thing was secretly brought to me, and mine ear received a little thereof. In thoughts from the visions of the night, when deep sleep falleth on men. Fear came upon me, and trembling, which made all my bones to shake (Job 4:12-14).

Job dreamt about fear, trembling, and the shaking of his bone when he was sick. Your physical condition goes a long way in influencing your dreams. That is why a banker would dream of counting money.

Power Against Dream Criminals

In the same vein, a post office staff may always dream of letters and stamps. You do not need to bother about these types of dreams. They only reflect your physical or emotional condition.

However, there is a class of dreams which should attract the attention of everyone. This class of dreams has ruined many people's lives. In particular, I am talking about SATANIC DREAMS.

A dream could come from the devil. Demons have infiltrated the lives of men and women through dreams. This is the area I really want to explore in this book.

THE DEVIL'S MOTIVE

The strategy of the devil is to cause calamity and destruction. His purpose is to inflict sickness on people, terrify men and make evil covenants with innocent souls. His sole aim is to kill and destroy. He also attempts confusing men and makes them to take wrong decisions.

The devil is a deceiver. He deceives through dreams. He gives people confusing images in their dreams. He might make a person see a man with a white garment in the dream and make him to conclude that God is speaking to him.

This reminds me of a brother who was praying and all of a sudden, someone walked up to him and told him to stop praying. He was baffled when the personality added, "That prayer is too much." The brother paused and wondered why Jesus would ever ask him to stop praying. However, the brother looked closely and to his surprise, he found dirty spots all over the garment of the strange personality.

His eyes opened. Then the brother shouted:

"You are an agent of the devil. You are not from God!"

The white garment man disappeared. The devil was trying to deceive him. This is how the devil darkens the vision of many prophets. After such a deceptive vision, they generally relapse into strange doctrines. They go about saying, "God told me that I should not eat any food cooked by a woman. God also told me that I should tear up my Bible and eat it." You must be careful when you hear or see such things. The devil is always looking for people to deceive.

DIRECT SATANIC ATTACKS

Besides leading people into error and bondage through dreams, the devil also afflicts people directly. All the dreams about accidents, attacks, carrying loads, closed doors, youth growing old, chains in the neck, closed Bibles are all symbolic. They represent one form of satanic attack or the other.

If you also find yourself drinking concoctions or poison in your dreams, you are surely under attack.

Power Against Dream Criminals

If you dream of your property being confiscated or if you see a coffin in your dream, the devil is at work.

Those who dream of seeing themselves being lost in the forest, those who see black shadows in dreams and those who see people running after them are also experiencing some forms of satanic attack.

Again, if you find yourself screaming in your dream, something is surely amiss.

Those who are fond of eating assorted foods in the dream are most probably under attack.

So are those who see snakes, water, dead relatives, 'spirit husbands', 'spirit children' and masquerades.

These all have connotations in the spirit world. The devil uses them as points of contact.

The list is almost endless. The Bible talks of "depths of satan". The devil has many mysterious ways of afflicting people.

Sweating profusely in the dream, labouring as in pregnancy, serving food to people you do not know, attending strange meetings in the dreams, being attacked by crocodiles, cats, dogs and lions and other strange occurrences in dreams are all part of satan's method of enslaving and destroying people.

SPIRITUAL WEAPONS

When unchecked, satan uses the dream world to his advantage. He has a very subtle trick. What he does is that he allows two or three bad dreams to come to pass; then he proceeds to make people to believe that every bad dream must come to pass.

When such people come to me for counselling and prayer, they often tell me: "Sir, my case is very urgent. Whenever I have a dream, it always come to pass. I am afraid this dream will also come to pass."

It is clear that people with this kind of mind-set have been deceived by the devil. You must not allow the devil to deceive you. That is why you should learn how to make use of spiritual weapons.

Those who come under our teaching and ministration regularly are always taught the effective use of weapons of spiritual warfare. You need to know how to make use of the weapons which God has given you.

But what does the Bible say about these weapons?

> For the weapons of our warfare are not carnal, but mighty through God to the pulling down of strongholds (2 Corinthians 10:4).

Power Against Dream Criminals

THE NAME OF JESUS

The most powerful weapon which is available for our use against satanic dreams is the name of JESUS. The Bible says:

> The name of the LORD is a strong tower: the righteous runneth into it, and is safe (Proverbs 18:10).

No matter how terrible you are attacked in your dream, if you can still have the consciousness to call the name of Jesus, no power will be able to overcome you.

You can use the name of Jesus to overcome every satanic warfare in the dream. But if you call the name of Jesus and evil powers refuse to obey, then there is a sin in your life. Something is surely wrong somewhere. There is no other explanation. You cannot blame another person. Sin will render your prayer ineffective. You, therefore, need to know the power in the name of Jesus.

Perhaps, you are wondering: why is it that sometimes when I am dreaming, I do not even remember to call the name of Jesus? It is because the name of the Lord Jesus has not yet entered into your spirit.

If you keep on repeating a particular word or phrase for ten hours, you will discover that you might continue repeating the word when you are asleep, because it has entered into your subconscious.

If you are always calling the name of Jesus in real life, you will find it easy to call His name in your dreams. In the same

Power Against Dream Criminals

way, if you are always making use of bad vocabulary, you will need deliverance. But when your vocabulary is positive and words like: "Jesus, glory be to God, God is good and the goodness of the Lord" are always on your lips, you will repeat the same words in your dreams.

THE BLOOD OF JESUS

The Blood of Jesus is another weapon you can use against satanic dreams. This is clearly stated in the Bible:

> And they overcome him by the Blood of the Lamb, and by the word of their testimony; and they loved not their lives unto the death (Revelation 12:11).

The Blood of Jesus is a very powerful weapon. Remember, it is written:

> And the blood shall be to you for a token upon the houses where ye are: and when I see the blood, I will pass over you, and the plague shall not be upon you to destroy you . . . (Exodus 12:13).

THE FIRE OF GOD

The fire of God is another weapon against demonic dreams. This may sound like a strange weapon, but earnest students of the Bible and matured students in the school of spiritual warfare are conversant with this weapon. The Bible declares:

> For behold the LORD will come with fire, and with His chariots like a whirlwind, to render His anger with fury, and His rebuke with flames of fire (Isaiah 66:15).

Power Against Dream Criminals

The Bible also stated that God is a consuming fire. So it is clear that you can call the fire of God to consume, burn or roast all forms of satanic dreams. The Word of God is filled with wonderful revelations concerning our spiritual weapons. You need to search the Word of God for light and guidance. You also need to memorize scriptures to effectively deal with the enemy each time he comes against your life. There is no short cut to victory.

If you fail to learn enough scriptures, you might be confused at the hour of battle. It is never too late. You can start to memorize scriptures today. The average Christian ought to be able to recite at least fifty memory verses.

It is rather unfortunate that some people find it difficult to commit Bible verses to memory. Such people are, however, quick to memorize the wordings of worldly music. This is the work of the enemy.

ANGELS OF GOD

Another strange but powerful weapon which God has given every believer are angels. Angels play a prominent role in the battles which the believer faces. The Bible says:

> There shall be no evil befall thee, neither shall any plague come nigh thy dwelling. For He shall give His angels charge over thee, to keep thee in all thy ways (Psalm 91:10,11).

Again the Bible says:

Power Against Dream Criminals

Let them be confounded and put to shame that seek after my soul: let them be turned back and brought to confusion that devise my hurt: . . . Let their way be dark and slippery and let the angel of the LORD persecute them (Psalm 35:4-6).

Angels are part of our weapon for spiritual warfare. Some believers think that we should never fight against or deal with the enemy. Some people believe that we should just fold our hands since God knows how to give us victory. But there is nothing wrong if a Christian prays and commands that certain spirits should be bound. You have the weapons. Why not use them?

There is nothing wrong with commanding the thunder and the lightning of God to blast the enemies of your soul. This is a very effective weapon.

Also, there is nothing wrong if a believer commands that the whirlwind of God should scatter the enemy's devices against him/her.

There is nothing wrong if a believer chooses to apply the arrow and the spear of God against dark powers.

There is nothing bad, too, if a believer commands the tempest of God to deal with all satanic agents.

There is just nothing wrong with a believer who prays like the psalmist, especially after being harassed or attacked in a dream.

Power Against Dream Criminals

COSTLY IGNORANCE

There are weapons every believer who wants to enjoy personal victory must learn to use. This is very important for members of churches where almost nothing is said about spiritual warfare. Whether you like it or not, you have to fight battles.

If you despise the weapons of your warfare, you are seeking your defeat. You cannot give any excuse for your defeat. The weapons are there in the Bible. If your personal victory is important to you, you will thoroughly search God's word and make use of the weapons fashioned for you by God.

However, you must be ready to forget your traditional church beliefs and embrace the teaching on spiritual warfare. Some believers want to appear more righteous than God. But see what the Bible says:

> My defence is of God . . . and God is angry with the wicked every day. If he turns not, he will whet His sword; He hath bent His bow, and made it ready. He hath also prepared for him the instruments of death; He ordaineth His arrows against the persecutors (Psalm 7:10-13).

> The heathen are sunk down in the pit that they made: in the net which they hid is their own foot taken. The LORD is known by the judgement which He executeth: the wicked is snared in the work of his own hands . . . (Psalm 9:15,16).

> The wicked in his pride doth persecute the poor: let them be taken in the devices that they have imagined (Psalm 10:2).

Power Against Dream Criminals

Stir up thyself, and awake to my judgement, even unto my cause, my God and my Lord. Let them be ashamed and brought to confusion together that rejoice at mine hurt: let them be clothed with shame and dishonour that magnify themselves against me (Psalm 35:23,26).

We must learn to use the various weapons put at our disposal by God. Why? Sources of problems differ. Sources of attack also differ. But praise God! The Lord has given us all the weapons we would ever need for the battle of life.

USE APPROPRIATE WEAPONS

Although God has given us many weapons, certain spirits will respond to a particular weapon while another weapon may not have any effect over them.

This reminds me of the story of somebody I prayed for a long time ago. Before I prayed for him, somebody came and issued a command saying: "Fire of God, burn this evil spirit".

Another person got there and said: "No, that is not the right method". He then prayed: "The blood of Jesus! get into this situation".

Then the problem started. The person being prayed for began to speak Latin. Imagine a fourteen-year-old boy who has never gone outside the country speaking fluent Latin!

Power Against Dream Criminals

The boy later confessed that the spirit troubling him came from Rome. No wonder, he had killed his father and mother. This is why we must study the different methods of dealing with demonic problems.

Certain stubborn spirits may require a combination of weapons.

For example, if you had a dream in which somebody came to take your property away, you should command that the Holy Spirit should reach out for the robber. You should also command the thief to appear with your property. Then bind the spirit behind the thief. You can also release the thunder, the arrow and the sword of God into the body of the thief. You can ask that the arrow remains there permanently. Then, you should collect your property. Finally, cover your property with the blood of Jesus.

Perhaps, you dreamt of seeing masquerades, you can command the consuming fire of the Almighty God to roast the masquerades. You can also send them to the place of torment. The masquerade is an embodiment of evil spirits in our environment.

It is very easy to know when a dream is from God, or if it is from the devil. If a dream comes from God, you will be normal when you wake up, but if it is a satanic dream, mysterious things will begin to happen to you. It will be accompanied by feelings of confusion and emptiness. It will leave you unconscious.

Power Against Dream Criminals

However, if you are attacked in a dream, never panic. Do not be afraid. Immediately you are afraid, evil strategies will begin to work against your life.

Perhaps, you may wonder how I have been able to understand certain mysteries of satanic invasions through dreams. But I doubt if you will wonder how a tested war general has mastered warfare. You will surely not wonder how such an army general has succeeded in demonstrating a mastery over the position, the weapons and the strategies of enemy forces.

Again, the weapons of the army general may be strange to you, all the same, he knows that his terminologies are real. His experience, his endowments and his personal experience would have made him a veteran.

In the same vein, you should expect a servant of God who has been incubated and trained by God to understand the mysteries and the interpretations of demonic symbols used in dreams. As you go through the list of the following symbols and meanings, you may come across certain revelations which may not be familiar to you.

What you are about to discover will make you to be more conscious of the fact that the devil is a blood-thirsty warrior who also carries his battle to the realm of dreams. He does not care whether you are ignorant or not. And he will do everything to keep you ignorant as long as he can continue to cause havoc in every area of your life.

Power Against Dream Criminals

DREAM SYMBOLS

I have decided to outline some dream symbols and their meanings only to give you some basic knowledge of the workings of satanic dreams.

A lot of things in the areas of deliverance and spiritual warfare may appear unintelligible to the mind of man but nonetheless, many people are suffering untold agony from the hands of satanic agents who attacked them through dreams. Many people have personally come to see me to narrate how their problems started through some strange dream experiences.

By the grace of God, we have led thousands of people into deliverance and victory. We may not touch your particular experience in this booklet, but you will gain some helpful insights into how satan uses dreams to attack men and women.

DEEP AND MYSTERIOUS *dreams and their meanings*

- *Seeing stagnant water* - represents lack of the moving of the Holy Spirit and stagnant progress. Review your spiritual life and pray against the spirit of lukewarmness.

- *Dirty water* - represents the flesh and spiritual dirtiness.

- *Hair* - represents the glory of God. Therefore, removal of hair in any form should be aggressively addressed.

- *Begging for alms* - This is the plan of the devil to prevent the person from getting out of an unemployed state or poverty.

- *Travelling on an unending journey* represents unprofitable endeavours - Ask the Holy Spirit to terminate all unprofitable endeavours.

- *Being driven by unknown persons to an unknown destination* - This represents profitless and confused life. Ask the Holy Spirit to unseat all unprofitable drivers and make His way plain before your face.

- *Doors closing just before you enter; distribution of items finishing just before it is your turn,* etc. - This represents the spirit of "almost there". Begin serious warfare praying against blockages at the edge of miracles.

- The underlisted dreams indicate that you are under attack by the *spirit of poverty*:

Power Against Dream Criminals

— *spending money lavishly*

— *seeing yourself buying things in the market, especially after a physical financial breakthrough*

— *wearing of rags or tattered shoes*

— *walking about bare-footedly*

— *seeing onself begging for alms*

— *having wares or merchandise unsold*

— *seeing your property being auctioned*

— *seeing your pockets leaking*

— *lost substantial amount of money and never found it*

— *thieves breaking into the house stealing things*

— *victim of pickpockets*

— *seeing rats running about in your house*

— *seeing rats running into your body*

— *your properties go missing*

— *your bag or purse containing money is stolen*

— *you found yourself with counterfeit money*

☞ *Always sitting for examinations never finishing before the allotted time -*   Demonic stagnancy, frustration and

Power Against Dream Criminals

discouragement. Declare war on ungodly delays and command success into your handiwork.

☞ All the underlisted dreams are dreams of *defeat and backsliding*. You must declare war against all such dreams with prayer and fasting:

– *nightmares*

– *death or being buried*

– *idol-worship or consulting diviners or witch-doctors*

– *stammering*

– *having cancer or any other disease*

– *insanity*

– *loss of salvation*

– *a man getting married to a man*

– *weakness toward temptation*

– *compromising holiness*

– *consuming alcohol*

☞ If you find yourself losing much hair from your head in real life after a dream experience in which you found yourself in a barber's shop where your hair was barbed by force, it is an indication that your glory or your security is being removed. You have to go into spiritual warfare and recover

Power Against Dream Criminals

your hair. You also have to send fire to the barber's shop in the realm of the spirit.

- *If you find yourself carrying a basket on your head in a dream*, it is an indication of a satanic plan to make you suffer loss financially. You have to send the fire of God to burn the basket and recover your lost blessings.

- *If you see bats flying in your dream*, it suggests that the devil is planning to use hypocrites and pretenders against you. You have to bind the bat and ask that the power of God should descend and consume it.

- *Generally, the animals* which most people see in their dreams represent difficulty, hardships and trouble. You should either drive the animals away or decree their death.

- *Consuming alcohol in the dream* is a symbol of being under the influence of the spirit of confusion. You have to pray that you will vomit the alcohol. You also have to expel yourself from the school of confusion.

- *When a sister is getting engaged with an unknown man in a dream*, something is amiss. If she begins to commit fornication with a strange man in her dream, she, perhaps, unknown to her, has a spirit husband. Something must be done about such a strange dream. It must be stopped through violent prayer.

- *Dreams of being abandoned* indicate satanic plans to make you lose friends and favour and also making recovery

Power Against Dream Criminals

difficult. Refuse to be abandoned in Jesus' name and also claim back friends and favour.

- *Dreams having to do with abortion* indicate that the enemy is trying to steal something good from your life before the full manifestation of the particular thing. Rebuke the enemy and reject the abortion of good things.

- *Dreams of contacts with dead parents and ancestors* indicate serious physical and spiritual illnesses and evil spiritual carry-overs. Reject evil linkage, break all evil ancestral covenants and carry-overs.

- *Dreams of being attacked by armed men* indicate that you have serious spiritual battles to fight and there is the presence of serious obstacles to goodness. Ask the hosts of heaven to take up the battle. Call down the fire of God to destroy the evil army.

- *If you find yourself bleeding in your dream*, it means that something good is going to come out of your life. However, this may be gradual and it may eventually lead to the loss of life. You have to command that the spirit of God should heal the wound and that there should be restoration of the blood.

- *Supposing you see corpses in your dream*, you have to stand and pray against the spirit of death.

- *If you are always dreaming of seeing cobwebs all over the place*, it is a symbol of rejection. It means that the devil is trying

Power Against Dream Criminals

to render your life useless. You must send fire to the spots where the cobwebs are located and scatter the producers.

- *If you dream of seeing yourself putting on earrings* when you normally do not put them on, it is a symbol of the enemy's attempt to turn you into a slave. You have to command that the earrings should be removed and sent back to the sender.

- *Any type of wigs* which people place on their head in the dream is a symbol of false glory. It cannot last. You have to send fire to burn it and restore your normal hair.

- *If you see yourself handcuffed in a dream*, a curse is being place over your life. In addition, the enemy may be attempting to incapacitate your freedom or handiwork. You have to destroy the handcuff and return it to the sender.

- *If you frequently see yourself in funeral services*, the enemy is challenging you with the spirit of death. You have to disband the funeral service including the "pastor" who is conducting it. You should also withdraw yourself from the service. It is not of God. The people who are there are only pretending to be church members. They are all satanic agents.

- *Again, if you find yourself before great mountains which you are unable to climb*, it means that there are still obstacles for you to tackle spiritually. You have to use all available weapons until the mountain is destroyed.

Power Against Dream Criminals

- *If you find yourself in the court and you happen to be the accused*, it is also an indication that there are obstacles before you. You need to pray against the obstacles and disband the court.

- *If you see padlocks in your dreams*, it means that your blessings have been locked up. You do not need to ask for the keys. Ask for the fire of God to burn the padlocks.

- *If you see yourself in tattered clothes in your dreams*, it means that you are going to lose some good things. You should stand against such a dream The enemy has plans to put you to shame.

- *If you find crabs walking all over your body*, it shows that you are going to experience a retreat. It is a sign of going backward. You should stand against it.

- *If you find yourself drinking dirty water*, your spirit is being poisoned.

- *If you also dream about swimming in dirty water*, your spirit is also being poisoned. You must pray that the blood of Jesus should enter into the water. You should also command the water to dry up.

- *If you find yourself eating in the dream*, it signifies that the enemy wants to poison your spiritual life. They may even be distributing different parts of human flesh and you may receive it if you are dull spiritually. This is satanic.

Power Against Dream Criminals

- *If you find yourself drinking a red substance, you might be drinking blood. You have to ask the Holy Spirit to purge you immediately. You need personal deliverance. Those who eat "Fufu", "Eba", "Yam", etc, are eating terrible poison that can cause them terrible diseases. Eating sand or dust in dreams shows that the enemy is trying to cause heaviness in your spirit.*

- *If you find that you were climbing with difficulty until you woke up to discover that you were sweating, profusel y, you need to pray seriously. But if you find yourself climbing until you eventually succeeded, you should begin to praise the Lord. You are victorious. If you climbed and you could not succeed, you should pray fervently against defeat.*

- *If you drove your car in a dream in a traffic jam which stood still until you wake up, it is symbolic of a major attempt at hindering you from getting what God wants to give you. Ask the Holy Spirit to send His dispatch rider there and clear the way for you. This kind of dream reveals the devil's strategy against your life.*

- *If a person is carrying a big load on the head and he or she is sweating under the great burden*, it means a big load on the head of the one who dreamt about it whether he knows about it or not. Such a person must reject the load and ask the Holy Spirit to remove the load from his or her head. The person can also cover himself or herself with the Blood of Jesus.

Power Against Dream Criminals

☞ *If you find yourself somewhere and you are told: "Look! this load belongs to you"* and you struggle endlessly without being able to lift up the load, you need to pray fervently. It means that the devil does not want you to fulfill your responsibility.

☞ *If you find yourself cooking beans in a dream and you cook for hours on end without the beans getting done,* you should not take it lightly. It symbolises some hindrances to receiving your goodness. You should pray that the Holy Spirit should cook the food for you.

☞ *If you also find yourself travelling in your dream and the vehicle in which you are travelling breaks down, and you kept on repairing it, and in spite of your efforts you could not finish the repairs before waking up,* this is an attack on the wheel of your progress. You must ask the angels of God to repair the vehicle. You must also rebuke the enemy.

☞ *Any form of darkness* in the dream is ominous. It represents spiritual blindness. Those who have such dreams will not see where they are going. Likewise, if you enter a vehicle or an aircraft and you begin to ask: "Where are we going?" this indicates that the enemy has dispatched the spirit of uncertainty and confusion against the individual.

☞ *People often see themselves receiving gun shots in the dream .* Surprisingly, bullets actually enter their body. They often feel pains when they wake up. Gun shots are evidences of affliction or satanic attack. It may eventually result into

Power Against Dream Criminals

poverty or sicknesses. Demonic gun shots can easily be removed. You just remove the bullets in Jesus' name. Ask the angels of God to minister treatment to you, then fire back at the source of attack.

- *If you find yourself naked in a dream*, it is a sign of disgrace or insecurity. You must ask the Holy Spirit to clothe you and remove any object of disgrace from your life.

- *If you are putting on rags*, it is a sign of poverty and blindness. Also, if you dream of seeing yourself in chains, it is a sign of imprisonment.

- *Any form of theft in your dreams* has a deep spiritual meaning. You have to pray aggressively and claim back whatever is stolen, be it clothes, shoes, etc.

- *If you dream about people stealing your wedding dress*, it is an attack on your marital life. You must go into fasting and prayer very quickly and command the wedding gown to be returned. Then go ahead and claim God's promises for your marriage. Dreams of wedding gowns stained with blood or in rags should be aggressively dealt with.

- *If your Bible is stolen in a dream*, it is an attack on your spiritual power and ability. It is the devil's attempt to paralyse your spiritual life and eventually make you to backslide. You have to rise up and resist the devil. Pray that the Holy Spirit should return your stolen Bible and collect it by faith from the thief.

Power Against Dream Criminals

- *Dreams on getting confused* when you are supposed to share the word of God should be resisted violently.

- *Dreams concerning burglary* are spiritual attacks. You have to pray that all your property should be returned.

- *In Africa mythology masquerades* are the embodiments of all evil powers. It represents the depth of satanic power. Any form of attack by masquerades should not be taken lightly at all. Masquerades are sent by witchcraft spirits and other demonic spirits. Their purpose is to disgrace you and push you into restlessness. You have to rebuke them aggressively in Jesus' name. You must paralyse their powers and use your weapon against them.

- *If you also find yourself among lodge members or if you find yourself in the midst of all kinds of people dressed in the regalia of demonic or occultic people*, it means that even in the place where you were born, you are surrounded by demonic agents. You have to fight them by commanding the fire to consume those groups of demons. Also break every conscious or unconscious covenant formed by you or formed by someone on your behalf with evil powers.

- *Any attack by dogs, cats and crocodiles* should be taken seriously.

This reminds me of a member of our church who formed the habit of praying aggressively every time. She had heard this kind of teaching. She was, therefore, sufficiently enlightened.

Power Against Dream Criminals

One day she was on her bed at home when a cat jumped in from the window and alighted on her bed. The cat bit her leg. She cried in the dream and continued doing so until she woke up. Before she woke up from the bed, the cat jumped out of the window, but as it jumped out, one leg got stucked in the window. The cat struggled and struggled until it ran out through the window.

Then when she woke up, she made her first mistake. She went to the wrong person, the oldest woman living in the house and challenged her:

"Mama, my blood is bitter. If you are the cat which came to me in the dream, leave me alone. You better go and attack your own children."

The woman replied:

"I don't know anything about any cat. I don't know what you are talking about."

Immediately the sister got to her room, her legs started getting swollen until she could no longer walk. So the sister was rushed to the hospital.

A man of God went there and told her that her case is not for the hospital. She was taken back home. The man of God then anointed the leg with oil and prayed over it. The leg began to reduce to its normal size. The pastor who ministered to her also prayed that the arrow should go back to its sender or to wherever Jesus wanted it to go.

Power Against Dream Criminals

This sister was a nurse. She did not know what was really happening until she got to work and discovered that her assistant at work had a mysterious problem in one leg. This other nurse who was the brain behind the sister's attack in the dream was in a critical condition in the hospital.

The Christian sister demanded to see her assistant whom she learnt was sick. She got an equally mysterious answer. The sister's assistant had given an instruction that everyone should be allowed to see her except the Christian sister. It became clear that the assistant was the culprit. She was the one who came in the form of a cat to attack the Christian sister.

In any case the sister suffered because of her ignorance of the weapons of the believer's warfare. If she had used her God-given authority, she would not have been attacked at all.

- *If you dream and you see dogs licking your body*, you have to pray. This means you have sexual demons. You must go for deliverance if need be. Any dream concerning anybody who takes a whip and flogs you, should be taken seriously as well.

- *Any dream centered on receiving dirty or rough money* symbolises contermination of your finances. You have to resist and rebuke the spirit behind it and destroy the money.

- *If you find yourself in the market in your dream, just roaming about without even remembering what to buy and*

Power Against Dream Criminals

you ended up buying nothing, it is an evidence that you will be confused financially. You must stand against it as well as destroy the market and withdraw yourself from it.

- *Any dream concerning somebody cursing you*, shows that the devil wants to put you under affliction perpetually. It shows that there is an evil handwriting against you. You must nullify the curses through prayer. You must blot out the handwriting and pray that the curse should go back to the sender.

- *It is also demonic to have any form of sexual intercourse in the dream.* This is the demon called spirit husband or spirit wife. You have to rebuke him or her in the name of the Lord. Attack this spirit with all the weapons you know about. Bind and stop the spirit from visiting you again. But be sure you are not engaged in the sin of adultery and fornication. These two sins are fertilizers for spirit wives and husbands.

- *If you have ever discovered that anytime you want to touch or start something good, a particular dream comes up which always results in rendering all your efforts futile,* you are suffering from what we call: "The Demonic Stabilizer". The dream stabilises you and keeps you at the same level. You must use the weapon of praying and fasting. This stabilizing demonic influence may not affect your entire life, but it is a hindrance to your progress and fulfilment in life. The yoke behind it should be broken.

Power Against Dream Criminals

- *It is not good to find yourself amputated in a dream*. You should pray against the spirit of death, if you have had such an experience in your dream.

- *If you find yourself in a school which is not of God*, disband the school and remove your name from their register.

When you begin to have these types of dream and you are ignorant of their implications, you might suffer unnecessarily. If you dismiss satanic dreams with a wave of the hand thinking that they are harmless, you are only deciding to allow the devil to have his way in your life. You will do yourself a lot of good if you pray against all satanic dreams.

In conclusion, whenever you have any of these dreams, you must pray and handle such things seriously. Do not give room to the devil.

Be systematic in your dealings with satanic dreams. If you are a child of God, you are not supposed to experience satanic dreams, but if you have had them as a result of ignorance, carelessness or prayerlessness, you can experience total victory.

You may ask: "But I have had these types of dream for so many years without doing anything about it. Can I still rectify things and undo what Satan has done?" Yes you can.

I have good news for you. There is a glorious opportunity in the spiritual world which you need to know about. If you have a cassette player you would have discovered that there are two important functions; fast forward and rewind.

Power Against Dream Criminals

Do you know that you have facilities in prayer? Do you know that you can rewind your dream experiences back to your infancy through prayers? You can counteract the effect of all the dreams you had for the past ten, twenty or thirty years.

You can pray in this manner: "Father, in the name of Jesus, I reverse the effect of the negative dreams I had ten years ago. Any negative effect should be completely cancelled by the blood of Jesus. In Jesus' name, Amen."

If there are dreams you have forgotten, you can ask the Holy Spirit to bring the important ones to your remembrance. After recalling the dreams, you can then go ahead to cancel their negative impact upon your life.

A PRACTICAL SESSION

This chapter will not be complete without this practical session. The Bible says:

> But be ye doers of the word, and not hearers only, deceiving your own selves (James 1:22).

There is, therefore, no way your practical benefit from the content of this booklet can be guaranteed without carrying out the following instructions.

On the one hand, it is possible to read about great peace without experiencing any iota of peace. It is also possible to read about prosperity without experiencing it. In the same vein,

Power Against Dream Criminals

you can discover the secrets of satanic dreams and you can continue to suffer harassments, defeats, attacks and afflictions through dreams. But on the other hand, you can tell the devil: "Enough Is Enough".

You can tell him that you are done with satanic dreams. You can only do this effectively by taking the following steps:

ONE You must give your life to Christ and experience the new birth. When you take this step, you will experience a major lift from the level of defeat to the level of dominion. The Bible says:

> Who hath delivered us from the power of darkness, and hath translated us into the Kingdom of His dear Son: In whom we have redemption through His Blood, even the forgiveness of sins (Colossians 1:13,14).

TWO You must pray fervently as instructed below. Prayer changes things. Prayer can change your dreams, too. Significantly, prayer removes the hands of the devil from your dreams.

THREE. Get personal practical help. In most cases, you may need person-to-person counselling.

Thousands of lives have been transformed through counselling and prayer. We counsel and pray for people every week. Your spiritual problem is our concern. If you were attacked in your dream, never panic when you wake up.

Power Against Dream Criminals

Cooly and calmly, even if your body is vibrating with fear, take the offensive. Use the name of Jesus as your combination of shield and battering ram.

Plead the Blood of Jesus and claim protection against the hosts of darkness. Rebuke satan and take authority over him and his wicked followers in the name of Jesus. Be persistent.

ANY REGULAR DREAM SHOULD BE GIVEN PROPER ATTENTION.

It may be a pointer to the way of solution to a particular problem. Be assured that the devil and his cohorts are behind all the horrible experiences in dreams like eating with the dead, swimming in water, serving people you do not know, playing with snakes, marriage in the spirit world with unknown men or women, having children in the spirit world, having sexual intercourse with known or unknown partners, getting out of the body for meetings, forceful sex or feeding, regular drinking of red liquid, being on a throne with unknown or known faces worshipping or bowing down to you and presence in unholy parties etc.

PRAYER POINTS

1. Every dream attack against my destiny, fall down and die, in the name of Jesus.

Power Against Dream Criminals

2. Every power of darkness using my dreams to manipulate my destiny, loose your hold, fall down and die, in the name of Jesus.

3. My dream life, receive fire of God, in the name of Jesus.

4. My life will not follow any evil pattern, in the name of Jesus.

5. Every power of failure working in my dreams, fall down and die, in the name of Jesus.

6. Every power of demotion working against my destiny, fall down and die, in the name of Jesus.

7. O God arise and scatter every enemy of my prosperity, in the name of Jesus.

8
PARALYSING SATANIC ANIMALS

Power Against Dream Criminals

We are looking at a very interesting topic entitled "Paralyzing Satanic Animals."

In order to afflict human beings, evil powers also make use of animals. Through the activities of these satanic animals, a lot of lives have been caged. As you are reading this book therefore, I want you to exercise three things, holy anger, holy aggression and violent faith in order to uncage yourself.

A sister told me that a woman was trying to give birth to a baby in a hospital and it was a bit problematic. But as soon as she was delivered of the baby, a bird flew into the labour room and the nurses quickly caught it and caged it and immediately the bird died, the woman that gave birth also died.

That was not the shocking thing. When the husband of the woman came and heard that his wife was dead, he started rejoicing and thanking God. The nurses who were by now watching the man with disbelief enquired to know why he was acting that way. The man told them that since the day he married the woman, he had never known peace. The question is, who or what is that bird?

ANIMALS AS SYMBOLS

Throughout the Bible, God uses animals as symbols. For example, Jesus is referred to as the Lion of the tribe of Judah. The devil is referred to as the roaring vagabond lion.

Power Against Dream Criminals

While some animals in the Bible are symbols of holiness, others are symbols of uncleanliness, wickedness and iniquity.

For example, the dove which is a gentle and harmless bird represents the Holy Spirit.

The Lamb which represents our Lord Jesus Christ, is a sacrificial, patient, and harmless animal.

The eagle represents the mountain top life. Another question is, is it possible for an animal to carry demons? The Bible says yes, because in the book of Mark 5:10-12, it is written:

> And he besought him much that he would not send them away out of the country. Now there was there nigh unto the mountains a great herd of swine feeding. And all the devils besought him, saying, send us unto the swine, that we may enter into them.

Here, it is the demons that begged Jesus. They said, "Please, Sir, we want to enter into those pigs," and Jesus said, "Go," and they went. So it is possible for an animal to carry demons. It does not matter how small or big the animal is.

Normally, an evil spirit will prefer to live inside a human being because there they can express themselves better. But when this is not possible, they enter into animals.

If a spiritual animal has been used to wage a spiritual war against you, or a spiritual war was waged against you in your dream with an animal, then, you really have to pray seriously. If before you got born again, you are one of those that have

Power Against Dream Criminals

used animals to make "juju" (local charm), concoction or sacrifices, you have to pray now. If it was used to make sacrifices against you, whether you know about it or not, you have to pray too.

When you see an animal playing a negative role in your dream, you really have to pray about it.

If in your dreams, you see animals running after you, biting you or doing evil things, you need to know that those things are not ordinary, you really have to pray. If you do not experience all these, but an animal appears to you physically as a satanic agent, you also have to pray.

A Professor friend of mine brought out his cutlass because a cat was crying beside his house at night.

As he was about to use the cutlass on the cat, it rose on two legs and was begging him. He threw the cutlass at the cat, it landed where the cat was and entered into the ground, but the cat was still standing there. It was then he knew there was a problem. If satanic animals are working at the root of one's life, there will always be a problem.

A sister told me that when a person was born in her family, the first meat they would give to that person must be an elephant meat, in order to neutralize the terrible spirit of anger that runs in the family, otherwise, the person could destroy himself or herself because of this evil spirit of anger. So, the

Power Against Dream Criminals

elephant meat was to calm the spirit of anger down and keep it under control.

There are many people who get possessed with evil spirits transferred to them from their demonic household pets.

I consider it a very dangerous spiritual exercise when a believer just buys a bird puts it inside a cage and hangs it in the house just for the purpose of watching a caged animal and not for any other business.

Some people who sleep at night and see themselves swimming in the river, still compound their problems by going to buy an aquarium and put in their sitting rooms so that water spirits can have more power in their lives. If somebody is sacrificing animals on your behalf consciously or unconsciously, you need to pray very well.

A man came for counselling and by the time we finished praying for him and he stood up to go, there was a tortoise on his seat. So, I asked him how it got there? He explained that they used it to make some charms for him sometime ago. To him, he thought they just make the charm and threw the tortoise into the forest and it walked away. He did not know that the exercise had opened the door for the devil to put a spiritual tortoise into his life to slow down his progress.

But after the prayer, it came out physically. Many of us come from families where they worship idols and practise witchcraft. So, every year we have to kill one thing or the other. When

Power Against Dream Criminals

you do things like that, you come under the attack of spiritual animals.

Not only this, whatsoever the animal represents, will be happening in your life. Look back and you will see the truth in what I am saying. The Bible says, "My people are destroyed for lack of knowledge."

There are some people who consume fetish things and the animals used to prepare them will be working against them.

What am I saying? I mean that it is possible that you have killed an animal to make "juju" (local charm) for yourself, and you now see them in your dreams. It may have happened in the past in any of the ways I have described. If that is your situation, you need to work hard to get rid of these things.

It is Christians who sometimes do not know what they are doing, but the enemy understands what he is doing all the time because he is very intelligent. What will destroy some people in 1998 must have been planted in them in 1980. It will just hide in them until the time when the demonic whistle will sound and it will start to work. The person will not understand what is happening.

SATANIC ANIMALS

Let us now examine these animals and how they operate.

Power Against Dream Criminals

The Ant - The first animal that the enemy uses and which has created a lot of problems in the lives of so many people is the ant. Sometimes when prayers are hot, some people will be feeling things running all over their bodies like small ants.

Now, let us take a look at the life of the ant so that we can understand it better.

The ant lays up all sorts of food. It prepares the soil for crops because of the way it feeds.

It also helps to free the ground of weeds.

When it is raining, ants know how to fortify their passages against rain and against their enemies.

They know how to close these passages every night and open them in the mornings.

They watch over their young with utmost care and provide food for them in abundance.

They are very wise and very hard working.

They are always busy. You will hardly find an ant standing idle, it must be busy doing something.

What does this refer to in the spirit?

It refers to highly efficient enemies, organized in a network against a person. So, if you start praying and notice that things are running all over your body, those are the demonic ants and you have to fight against them.

Power Against Dream Criminals

The Bat - The bat is a half beast, half bird. It is listed amongst the unclean animals in the Bible.

It has claws in the hands by which it attaches itself to things. It is a nocturnal animal. Most people do not know that bats are blind. They move by their ears.

What does this mean in the spirit?

It refers to spiritual blindness and death. No matter what you tell people that are being attacked by the spirit of the bat, they will just refuse to see the light of the gospel. They are the kind of people who combine both Christian and world activities together. Even when such people are under crisis they will still refuse to run to Jesus, no matter how much they are suffering.

Therefore, attacks from physical and spiritual bats should be taken seriously. When bats are attacking a person, it means that evil powers are trying to blind the person's spiritual eyes and they can do terrible havoc. If they are always paying a person a regular visit, the person should start praying against the spirit of death and hell.

The Bees - If you study the life style of bees, you will find out that they have a queen, something like a king, officers, soldiers, and servants, meaning that they operate a kingdom.

But the bad thing about bees is that they dislike strangers and are always unhappy with intruders.

They have very bad temper.

Power Against Dream Criminals

All those who have been unlucky to offend them have either landed in the hospital or somewhere else for treatment. When they are attacking their enemies, they cooperate very well. They sting people and cause a lot of harm.

Deut. 1:44 says:

> And the Amorites, which dwelt in that mountain came out against you and chased you, as bees do, and destroyed you in Seir even unto Hormah.

So the Lord likened the way the Israelites were pursued to how bees operate.

What does it mean in the spirit?

It means a highly organized, angry and raging army. It is very bad for a person to be pursued or stung by bees in the dream.

The Dog - We all know what a dog is. They even eat their own vomit and the person who is being attacked may be torn into pieces unless he or she runs away.

Dogs can be very greedy, selfish and quarrelsome, and they are known for their sexual perversion.

So, when you are dreaming of dogs attacking you, running after you or you see dogs running around you physically, it is the spirit of worldliness, the spirit of Egypt, the spirit of sexual perversion and the spirit of impurity. It is not a very good

Power Against Dream Criminals

thing for dogs to pursue a person. If it has ever happened to you, you really need to pray hard.

The Flies - The fly is the adult of the maggot. They love decayed things. Beelzebub which is another name for the devil in the Bible means the 'Lord of the flies'. What does this mean in the spirit? It signifies the spirit of decay.

If you have a vision or a dream, and you find flies surrounding your Bible, you need to pray hard. It is an attack by tormentors. It is the spirit of decay and we must stand against it.

The Fox - The fox is known for its remarkable craftiness and it lives in holes. When a person is being pursued by a fox in the dream, it shows that an evil wisdom is working against the person.

The Frog - It acts without thinking. Hypocrisy is its worst form.

The Goat - The goat is destructive and unintelligent. It generally has to be kept from mischief. It is stubborn and wild.

So when somebody is being attacked by this animal, it signifies stubborn and persistent attacks by evil forces and they must be angrily dealt with.

If you have made sacrifices with goats before, it will open the door for stubborn and persisted forces to be attacking you.

Power Against Dream Criminals

The Lizard - The lizard quickly jumps at the slightest movement or noise.

It is afraid of practically everything. If you have contact with this kind of creature, it represents the spirit of fear.

It can also be responsible for the spirit of insanity. Sometimes when you pray for people with mental trouble and lizards are pulled out of their heads, they get healed instantly.

The Scorpion - This is a very dangerous animal which is black in colour. It is malicious to the extreme and inflicts great pain.

What does it represent?

It represents the spirit of affliction and pain. They do not recognize friends. Ezekiel 2:6 says,

> And thou son of man, be not afraid of them, neither be afraid of their words, though briers and thongs be with thee, and thou dost dwell among scorpions: be not afraid of their words, nor be dismayed at their looks, though they be a rebellious house.

The Lord told Ezekiel that He was living among sorpions. In the book of Luke 10:19, the Lord told us that He has given us power to thread upon serpents and scorpions.

The Serpents - Serpents move on their bellies because they do not have legs. They are extremely crafty and wild.

Power Against Dream Criminals

Readers of the book of Genesis knows that the serpent was the most beautiful of all the animals and the fact that it moves on its belly as a result of the curse God placed on it, means that it used to walk with its legs before.

When under attack, the serpent guides it's head with extreme care. Why does it do that? It does so because it's heart is very near to the head, so, it tries to stop you from touching it.

The easiest way to kill it is to crush or cut off its head. What does it represent in the spirit? It is the power of darkness in all its ramification. They represent the fallen spirits. It was through the serpent that the devil dislodged, defiled and utterly destroyed the tenants in the garden of Eden who had just been introduced into the world, a world that he wanted for himself.

The serpent is a symbol of lies and deception. He tries to deceive people and dislodge them from their place of blessings and to also defile them. It is not something to take lightly, whether in the physical or spiritual.

A sister was promoted to a high position in her place of work and her colleagues threatened to get rid of her, but thank God she is a Christian and she knows her authority.

One day as she was sitting on her table, suddenly, she felt something cold on her leg. When she looked, it was a snake. She screamed against the serpent saying, "I bind you in the name of Jesus." No weapon that is formed against me shall prosper, etc." Immediately, she said that, it was as if an electric

Power Against Dream Criminals

shock went through the body of that snake. It became afraid, left her leg and stretched out on the floor and just died like that. It was then she called in her messenger.

When he came into the place and saw the dead snake, he ran out, in fear. As in this case, when a physical serpent is sent against somebody and the sender decides to inject his own human spirit inside the serpent, the person dies as soon as the snake is killed.

The Rat or the Mouse - It is forbidden as food in the Bible. Rats are very destructive. So, if you have been seeing rats and mice in the dream, they represent the spirit of poverty and wastage.

I will not be surprised if a person who sees rats and mice in the dream becomes poor because that is what they are meant to do.

The Spider - This is a tiny animal which is remarkable for spinning webs for the purpose of catching it's preys. No matter how well you clean your house, after a while, you always find a spider in one corner or the other. That is why we preach at M. F. M., that when you destroy the spider, there will be no cobweb.

What does it mean in the spirit?

It is the spirit of blockage, greed, selfishness and jealousy.

Power Against Dream Criminals

When the Mountain of Fire and Miracles Ministries Abeokuta branch, took off, some young girls who came for counselling said something quite strange. They said that they see cobwebs during the day around them and sometimes they used their hands to remove them, but nobody else saw the cobwebs except them.

It means that a demonic spider was dispatched against them. They make a person's life to be stale. They put people's lives on the shelf through this means.

The Pig - A pig is a very dirty, destructive and extremely gluttonous animal. They eat anything, including faeces and their young ones.

They are noisy, fearful and sexually uncontrollable.

What does t mean in the spirit?

It represents the terrible spirit of destruction, and if they attack a person in the dream, it can result in insanity, because the person will lose the normal inhibitions.

Tortoise - This is one of the slowest animals created by God. It sticks its head out of its shell only to withdraw it when trouble comes. The Bible refers to it as an unclean animal.

What does it mean in the spirit?

It means retardation. People under the attack of the spiritual tortoise accomplish very little. Such people dodge

Power Against Dream Criminals

responsibilities. It also represents the spirit of laziness and procrastination. We need to pray against it.

Worms - It is difficult to find a normal human being who gets fascinated by worms. They are destructive and signify the spirit of destruction and poverty.

They are also demonic parasites.

They need to be paralysed. If you have been seeing yourself in the dream eating worms, vomiting worms or worms moving about in your body, you need to pray hard.

The Cock or the Hen - A cock grows generally to herald dusk or dawn.

It is sexually aggressive.

The mother hen too, sometimes loses quite a lot of its chicks to death in so many ways.

What do they signify in the spirit?

It means periodic wave of trouble which follows a particular timetable. It also signifies the inability to fly high in life.

It is the spirit of the tail. The hen picks dirty things from the ground and eats remnants.

So, if your parents always kill a hen or cock for you periodically, you really need to pray.

Power Against Dream Criminals

The Owl - The owl is an unclean and very strange bird. All its habits are repulsive. Some people call it the "night monster" while others call it the "bird of death". It is not the kind of thing you see around and you start smiling. It is not the kind of thing you see around and you pray one or two minutes prayer and assume that it is okay.

Sometimes, you need to do a night vigil when you see this strange bird around. The bird is supposed to go to only lonely places. But when it now comes to residential places, something is wrong. The bird looks very old with strange eyes. What does it mean in the spirit? It signifies the spirit of death and hell, the spirit of false knowledge and the spirit of evil wisdom.

The Vulture - The vulture is an unclean bird which is always associated with dead animals.

It eats dead and decayed creatures. It is always hovering around the dead to eat their flesh.

Sometimes, they feed their children with their own blood. They fly rapidly and their power of smell and vision is very sharp at picking evil things.

What does this mean in the spirit?

It signifies suicidal tendencies.

Many years ago, when I was a biology teacher in a secondary school, I was the master on duty on a particular week and a girl came late. Normally, we close the gate at 8.00a.m. and if a

Power Against Dream Criminals

student comes late, he or she stands in the center of the school, raises his or her hands up as a form of punishment for half an hour or so, before he or she is allowed to go into the class. So, I asked this girl why she came late. She said,

"Sir, this is the time I normally come to school."

I gave her the normal punishment and she refused to obey and told me that she wanted to go to her class.

When she saw that I was serious, she started obeying reluctantly and I ordered her to do it quickly.

But she did not listen. So, I took my cane and told her that I was going to give her six strokes of the cane. She laughed and said "Master, you must be new in this school." I said "what do you mean?"

"Nobody beats me, go and ask the last teacher that beat me what happened to him", she replied. Some of my students who love me so much, who saw me with a cane talking to this girl, rushed out of their classroom and said, "Biology master, do not touch that girl because she fainted the last time she was beaten and they had to bring her mummy from home, and she made so much trouble." I insisted on beating her and she said she would faint if I did.

So, I gave her six strokes of the cane but she did not faint. I said, "Now run to your class" and she did. There are many people like that who use fainting acts to control the whole house.

Power Against Dream Criminals

This is part of what the vulture spirit does. Whenever a vulture is hovering around, know that the spirit of death is around the corner. When you are in the desert and a camel is getting tired, you would see vultures appear, waiting for the camel to fall down and immediately the camel drops dead, they jump on it.

WHAT IS THE WAY OUT OF ALL THESE?

Repentance - If you have wrongly used animals in an ungodly way, whether consciously or unconsciously, you have to repent.

Ask for forgiveness for giving the enemy a foothold to be attacking you. When there is an attack of the enemy, the first place that wise people look at is inside, not outside.

Take an inventory of all your activities and revelations so that you know what to attack.

Summon every associated spirit and decree the fire of judgement upon them.

Despatch them back to the sender, so that the sender would know that you are not the kind of person they send those kinds of things to.

Pray to repair what they have destroyed or displaced.

Power Against Dream Criminals

Barricade your life now with the blood of Jesus, the fire of the Holy Ghost and the word of God, so that they do not mess up with you again. It is time to destroy every satanic animal, whether the one that has worked in the past, the ones working now or the ones programmed to work in the future. Do not take anything for granted. Remember to pray with holy anger, holy aggression and violent faith.

PRAYER POINTS

1. Every spirit associated with any satanic animal delegated against me, appear now, in the name of Jesus.

2. You spirits gathered together, receive the fire of judgement, in the name of Jesus.

3. Every rage of the enemy against my life, quench, in the name of Jesus.

4. Every stubborn oracle divining against me, be frustrated, in the name of Jesus.

5. Every stubborn familiar spirit, working against me be disgraced, in the name of Jesus.

6. Let divine earthquake shake down the foundation of every satanic prison, in the name of Jesus.

9
PARALYSING SATANIC MINISTERS

Power Against Dream Criminals

MINISTERS OF LIFE AND MINISTERS OF DEATH

The Bible makes it clear that there are only two types of ministers in the scriptures; these are those that minister life, and those that minister death. Therefore, there can only be two kinds of ministries; the ministry of life and the ministry of death.

The ministry of death can also be rightly called the ministry of destruction. This is why all careful readers of the Bible will discover, that there is so much violence in the Bible, beginning from the first page.

Why is the Bible violent? It is a book of life, and a spiritual war manual. The truth is certain that when there is no war, there cannot be peace. Jesus fought a terrible war all the way to redeem us and that war was so serious that when He was there on the cross, all the angels ran away, even the father turned His back and He cried out, "My Father, My Father why has thou forsaken Me?" He was in the midst of serious warfare. So, for us to be redeemed, terrible wars had to be fought.

Sometimes, when there is no war, there cannot be peace. When you throw two people into the boxing ring and boxer 'A' knocks out boxer 'B' in the very first round, when next you invite boxer 'B' to fight with boxer 'A', he will think twice.

These people called the ministers of destruction are so violent and senseless, and are ready to use any method to destroy their victims. Therefore, for a minister of life to stop the minister of destruction, there is no simple method to use. He too has to employ violence.

If somebody is chasing another person with a cutlass and the person being chased wants to stop the pursuer, there is no gentle way of doing this. He too has to be violent. This is why the minister of life must also learn how to destroy.

I John 3:8 tells us that,

> He that committeth sin is of the devil, for the devil sinneth from the beginning. For this purpose the son of God was made manifest, that he might destroy the works of the devil.

So, Jesus is a destroyer, but what He destroys is the works of the devil. Praise the Lord! However, satanic ministers minister destruction.

THE SATANIC MINISTERS

Then, you may ask the question - who are theses so called satanic ministers? I will give you various examples.

Drinkers of blood and eaters of flesh - These are those who use human blood to serve their own purpose. They join the nursing and medical profession just to drink blood. Their duty is to feed the blood bank of the enemy. There are those who consume human flesh and when they start with a person, there is no medical science that can help, because the microscope to

Power Against Dream Criminals

detect their activities has not yet been manufactured. As a matter of fact, the medical doctor to treat the effect of their activities is not yet born. To make it worse, these eaters of flesh and drinkers of blood are all over the place.

Ancestral strongmen - They are attached to various families from the past, and they stay there and keep following people about. They also, are satanic ministers and they minister destruction.

Dream manipulators - They come to a person's dream and manipulate the dream against the person, do evil through the dream and eventually wreck the person's life. They do a lot of wreckage in people's lives. That is why you should pray that the Lord should lift you up to the rock that is higher than you, and higher than your enemy.

Satanic wives and husbands - It can really be very wicked when somebody is married in the spirit world to a wife or husband. If a man is married to a spirit wife, the proper wife will not be able to stay in that house.

Do not think it is only the women have the problems of moving from one husband to another. There are many men too, who cannot retain a wife, simply because they have another wife in the spiritual world. This spirit wife will show the earthly wife hell. The same applies to spirit husbands. A lot of women have been married off to these satanic husbands. Some have their wedding rings, materials etc. given to them by these husbands.

Power Against Dream Criminals

For some, it is so bad, that they take you to the house where this spirit husband lives, show you their children, which they can see physically, but you cannot see them. They have a family that is seemingly happy, but in reality it does not exist.

When people see them, they admire them believing that they are wonderful, happy families, whereas the husband is not a normal human being. There was a case like that, which I knew of. After the sister had prayed the MFM prayers, she got home and could not find any trace of her husband again. The husband's car, the children, and every other thing had disappeared. She met an empty flat. This is a true life story. It was then this sister who was about 37 years started to look for a husband to marry.

When she started coming to MFM meetings, the husband warned her to stop and that if she continued, and gave her life to Christ, she would not meet him at home again.

Strange children - These are planted into families and their duty is to supply information on various good things happening in the family, so that they will be destroyed. These children, instead of sleeping normally, chat with strange spirits in their sleep in audible voices, even as they put their legs on the wall. Only one of them in a family is enough to turn everybody in the family into paupers, unless some people in the family have the fire of God. I do not say people who carry Bibles, because a lot of people carry Bibles around but do not have fire in their spirit.

Power Against Dream Criminals

Satanic spies - They also come to spy in order to report the good things happening in people's lives to their counterparts. They are ministers of the devil.

Satanic equipment and gadgets - These are also satanic ministers. A lot of people do not know that the medicated glasses that some people put on are sometimes not ordinary. They can see a lot of hidden things with these glasses. They X-ray people's lives, their internal organs, their state of health etc. They can monitor everything with these glasses.

Somebody brought a padlock here and we asked what it was for and she said she had locked somebody up with it before then.

We asked her to open the padlock and she opened it. We then asked if the person she locked up was then free, she said not yet, because there were fifteen other padlocks that she locked up on the same person. So, this person will not know why his prayers are taking so long, why his deliverance could succeed in breaking only ten of these evil padlocks. All these equipment and gadgets are instruments in the hands of the ministers of the devil.

There was a wedding where the bride and bridegroom were joyfully dancing in the church. But there was a woman waiting for them at the front of the church. And while they were dancing, and sweating, she wiped their faces with a handkerchief. By the time they got to the reception hall, they could not see anything again. Then they remembered that a

Power Against Dream Criminals

woman used a handkerchief to wipe their faces in the church. The handkerchief was not an ordinary handkerchief. It was a satanic equipment.

Counterfeit angels - They are on assignment every day. They go about collecting sacrifices at cross-roads and distributing these to people. They prepare satanic foods for all kinds of celebrations, e.g., birthdays, burials, etc. These evil people celebrate 21st birthday three times in a year and people attend the parties, to eat and drink. Many foolish people are deceived when a woman of 75 claims to be 40, and she now celebrates a fake 40th birthday and people go there to eat and to drink.

These counterfeit angels usually lead people to such gatherings, and the Bible tells us that angels of darkness, sometimes counterfeit as angels of light, because they want to deceive the elect.

Diviners - These include herbalists, 'babalawos' etc. who divine for people. They relate and communicate with demons that inhabit their objects of divination like cowries, shells etc. They hear the demons but the patient would not. When they divine ten correct things, they add twenty curses on it and these curses go to the 'patient'. This is the lot of people who visit diviners. They are satanic ministers.

Fake ministers - These carry Bibles, but they are fake. There are so many of them around these days. They engage in devilish and questionable acts, e.g. some of them lock some

Power Against Dream Criminals

people up in their so-called churches, tell these people to fast for 21 days and during the 21 days, they must not greet anybody neither must they read the Bible. Sometimes they transfer themselves into people's dreams, and cause havoc to such people in these dreams.

Operators of evil machines - They have evil machines in the spirit world and they use them to monitor people's lives. They are like satellite systems.

Evil advisers/evil counsellors - They advise and counsel people against their goodness. They persuade people so strongly that they follow their unprofitable advice.

They are the ones who go to women in their husbands' homes and encourage them to be stubborn and rebellious. They instigate wives against their husbands just to break their homes, whereas, they worship their own husbands at home.

Distributors of sickness and poverty - They are satanic agents walking about, distributing poverty and sickness all over the place, to different people. They are all around us.

Problem expanders - They specialize in turning small issues to big problems. Something that should be solved quietly is unnecessarily expanded and blown up to terrible proportions.

Occultists/cult members. If you belong to any secret society, you are constructing spiritual coffins for yourselves and your children. They do not prosper anyone. Their members may

Power Against Dream Criminals

seem to be prospering but eventually, the reverse is the case. They are satanic ministers.

If your father belonged to any of these funny societies, but is now dead, and he used to like you specially, he has probably submitted your name to them, and you will really need to pray, to cancel their records.

Evil broadcasters - They never mind their business. They keep peddling rumours from one place to another and relay other people's activities to others without being asked.

Satanic caterers - They cook both in the dream and in the physical. When we were very young, we used to get really upset with our mother, because when people bring big bowls of rice, with big pieces of meat, she will collect it from them, but will not allow us to eat them. The food would then be flushed down the toilet at night. We used to be annoyed because we felt it was wastage, we did not understand.

Then, one day, somebody brought this kind of rice and for some reasons, we forgot it somewhere, and when we came the next morning, there were two large worms playing in it. If somebody had eaten it, such a person would have gotten contaminated.

Somebody also shared an experience with me. Somebody brought food to their house for them to eat, but for some reasons, they fed their dog with it and the dog ran mad instantly, and started to look for whom to bite. Suppose human

Power Against Dream Criminals

beings had eaten the rice, what would have happened? There are many cases like this.

Blood hunters - They always go about wishing that vehicles will somersault or that bloody accidents will happen. They hunt for blood for the satanic blood bank. They are satanic ministers.

Sperm hunters - These hunt for sperm. This is a warning to men who are careless and undisciplined. They should be careful, because there are people hunting for their sperm and when they get the sperm and store them in their bank, the victim's finances are in trouble.

Satanic messengers - They carry evil messages all over the place.

Satanic soldiers - They defend evil all about.

Satanic musicians - They sing terrible music to confuse people. These kinds of music are made under the influence of drugs.

Satanic teachers - They are many in our midst. They teach people all sorts of satanic tricks to get what they want.

Satanic advertisers - They sell and advertise all kinds of things ranging from human bones to vulture heads. Some people go to buy leaves from them to cure malaria and then, they get more problems added to the malaria.

Power Against Dream Criminals

Impersonating the dead - These ones move about, appearing as the dead.

Evil pursuers - They pursue people about. They sometimes become stubborn because they have been promised promotion in their group, if they get the victim, or punishment, if they fail.

Bondage distributors - They distribute bondage to unsuspecting people. There are so many of them at the markets. They sell trinkets, Jewelleries, cosmetics, paint, attachment, artificial nails, all of which are bondage.

Funny enough foolish people buy from them and put them on. They do not know when these things are pursuing them. The pursuers are within the things they have bought with their money.

You might want to ask, "How does God deal with these satanic ministers? Does He just leave them alone or does He appeal to them to stop their activities?" No, God has His own aggressive method of dealing with satanic ministers.

I have given a general view, but when we come down to the black man's environment, the case is different. If you are from Nigeria, you will have to multiply all that I have told you by seven. One more thing I would like you to know, before I go ahead on how God deals with these satanic ministers, is that the world of the spirit is an interesting place.

Those that people think are witches, actually are not witches, but those that people never really expect to be witches are the witches. This is why sometimes God closes people's eyes so that they would not see. If they are opportune to see the spirit world, they might collapse or faint from shock.

GOD'S METHODS OF ADDRESSING SATANIC MINISTERS

By confusing their tongues - In Genesis Chapter 11 verse 7, it was revealed, how God confused the tongues of the people constructing the Tower of Babel. They could no longer understand one another's language. This resulted in confusion, and they could no longer work together, neither could they take counsel together. The whole purpose was defeated. So, a prayer point like, "Let satanic ministers and vessels working against me drink the water of confusion" is very terrible for the enemy.

Another one is "O Lord arise, and scatter the language of the enemy." These prayer points send confusion into the camp of the enemy.

Sometime ago, I was invited to preach in a place and a nice girl was singing praise and worship. She sang very well, danced very well and did all kinds of things.

After the preaching, I said let us pray and called the first prayer point: "Let the enemies of my soul receive confusion sevenfold." As they started praying, something strange

Power Against Dream Criminals

happened. Somebody swam from her seat in the congregation, on hard concrete to me at the front by the pulpit. She was so confused, she thought she was in the water, whereas she was swimming on hard concrete.

When I looked at her face, I discovered that she was the same lady that led the praise and worship. This is what happens when confusion enters into the camp of the enemy.

When confusion entered into the camp of the enemies of Elisha, they came to Elisha telling him that they wanted to arrest Elisha, not knowing that he was the man they were looking for. He then informed them that Elisha was not there. He instructed them to follow him and he ended up arresting them all. It is also like the prayer point which says, "Every evil imagination against me should fail". As you know, it is imagination that brings forth action.

So, before the enemy can put something into action against you, it must first of all be in his imagination. When you now command that imagination to fail, then the action too will fail.

When you pray this kind of prayer and the witch that has planned to take your case to the witchcraft meeting gets to the meeting, her imagination will fail. She will not remember anything again and she will even be punished for wasting the time of other witches.

He uses the rain of fire and brimstone - He did this for people that were against him at Sodom and Gomorrah in

Power Against Dream Criminals

Genesis Chapter 19. Also, Elijah, in 1 Kings Chapter 18 called down fire on some satanic ministers.

Anti-Egyptian techniques - If you have studied the way the Israelites came out of Egypt, you will know that God started with his arsenals in order of preference and increased gradually in power at different stages.

All the ten plagues were aimed at the gods of Egypt, because the Egyptians worshiped practically anything. In Egypt of those days, a cow was regarded as a sacred animal and treated as such. God disgraced all the gods of the Egyptians. This experience shows us that God has no gentle methods of dealing with satanic ministers.

Compulsory and forceful burials - In Numbers 16, Moses commanded the ground to open up and swallow, and it happened.

Withering of hands - When people point evil hands against the children of God, such hands wither. You will find an example of this in 1 Kings Chapter 1. I pray today, that every evil hand pointed at you shall wither, in Jesus' name.

Blindness - In 2 Kings Chapter 6, verse 19, Elisha put blindness on all the armies of Syria.

Paul, also, in Acts Chapter 23, asked Bar-Jesus to be blind.

When the enemy is blind, he is handicapped. If a witch tries to fly without eyes, it will result in a fatal accident.

Power Against Dream Criminals

Angelic warriors - God uses angelic warriors like we find in 2 Kings Chapter 19, one angel was sent to the armies of Senacherib and he destroyed the whole of the Assyrian army.

Terrifying noises - God also uses terrifying noises like you will find in 2 Kings Chapter 7. The Syrians heard terrifying noises and they ran away.

By throwing divine stones - God throws divine stones. You might be wondering if this is true, but in Joshua Chapter 10, verse 11, it was recorded thus:

> And it came to pass, as they fled from before Israel, *and* were in the going down to Beth-horon, that the LORD cast down great stones from heaven upon them unto Azekah, and they died: *they were* more which died with hailstones than they whom the children of Israel slew with the sword.

When God throw stones, no one can dodge them.

Personal destruction - God uses the method of personal destruction. In 2 Chronicles Chapter 20 verse 2, we read that when the children of Israel were singing, the enemies destroyed one another.

When you begin to walk the way the Lord wants you to, the people who have grouped together to fight you will fight one another and you will be the one to settle them.

Worms of destruction - God uses what is called worms of destruction. As it is recorded in Acts Chapter 12, God allowed satanic worms to eat up Herod. This can still happen today.

Power Against Dream Criminals

By pronouncing curses - God pronounces curses on satanic ministers, when He has business to do and some satanic ministers are trying to hinder Him.

MINISTERS OF LIFE

As we have these satanic ministers, so do we have others who minister life. Those who minister life are those who received spiritual power from God from on high, and transfer them to men or use them to bless others. This is why the Bible says "How beautiful are the Path of they that preach the gospel of peace."

Even if a head had been polluted by the enemy, and the beautiful feet of the gospel preachers get there, the head will be washed clean.

When Philip got into Samaria, there was much joy in the city. Likewise, the devil has his own vessels, that he sends to people. They are his own ministers. He puts dangerous weapons to be used against the people on their bodies.

Sometimes, He sends them to Churches to cause confusion, to homes to wreck them, and to shops to spoil things. People receive messages from the enemy and put their safety in jeopardy. It is a pity that human beings submit themselves for use by the devil.

Power Against Dream Criminals

When some sicknesses are healed and gone, satanic ministers bring them back.

I remember a gory thing which happened in Uganda. A man took his wife to a herbalist and the herbalist told them that both the man and his wife would be pregnant. The husband insisted that he wanted only the wife to get pregnant but the herbalist refused. Then the man agreed that they would both get pregnant, and the herbalist went to work.

The woman got pregnant and at the same time the husband too got pregnant. As the pregnancy grew, the man's stomach got bigger. When the woman went into labour the man too went into labour. But the man died soon afterwards.

That was the handiwork of a satanic minister. Many of them are still in the business of destruction today. The terrible thing about them is that they also come to sympathize with their victims.

A brother who was driving his car had to pass across a railway line. But as soon as he drove unto the rail line his car stopped. A train was then approaching. He did not know what to do again. He tried to push the car, but the car refused to move. He then jumped out of the car and was trying to push it. As an old man saw him struggling with the car, he shook his head and said there was something else to it. Satanic ministers were at work.

Power Against Dream Criminals

Many people that you see dressing haggardly on the streets to make people to laugh are satanic ministers. Once people begin to laugh at them, such people run into problems.

There are thousands of satanic ministers in market places, cinema houses, night parties, hotels, club houses etc. Many of the so-called prophets, prophetesses and holy-mothers, are demon possessed people. Many of them possess snake and witchcraft spirits and only prophesy what they have already discussed and agreed on at witchcraft meetings. Their holding of the Bible is just a camouflage.

How can a prophet give somebody black soap for a special bath? Where is it written in the Bible that a person needs to bath by the stream before God answers his prayers? Why should prayers be classified into special or ordinary prayers? Why should people be praying with sand?

You must really think about these things.

Perhaps, sometimes in the past, when you were praying at night you felt your head swelling up, or a paralysing shock taking over your body, or you felt that somebody was choking you, or a cold feeling from your head to your feet, or a sudden intense fear inside your spirit, shaking your heart. You need to pray seriously because these are manifestations of the visitation of satanic ministers.

Your prayer point must be, "Woe unto the vessel of the enemy" I will share a testimony with you.

Power Against Dream Criminals

Once upon a time, there were three boys who used to pray lackadaisical prayers, in a very tired mood. These prayers were very short - and powerless. They did this for so long, day in day out. After sometime, they started seeing scratches on their bodies, and the scratches became worse daily. Then they held a meeting and decided to increase their prayer power and time.

On the first night, they prayed for one hour and in the morning the scratches reduced, but they were still there.

On the second night, they prayed for three hours, and by the next morning there were no scratches.

On the third night, they also prayed for three hours and went to bed. A rat woke them up at night. It was running around their room. They chased the rat and killed it. In the morning an old man came to inquire from them if they had seen a rat. One of the boys then asked "Are you the rat?" The old man went back home and died.

If you have not yet given your life to Jesus Christ, and you are ready to do so now, place your right hand on your head and pray like this: "Lord Jesus, I come to you now and I confess my sins before you, forgive me all my sins. Jesus, come into my life. Take control of my life as from today in Jesus name. Amen."

Power Against Dream Criminals

PRAYER POINTS

1. Enemies from my place of birth, receive confusion, in the name of Jesus.

2. Let divine fire, and brimstone, baptise the camp of the enemy, in the name of Jesus.

3. Let the stubborn pursuers die in the red sea, in Jesus' name.

4. You ground, open and swallow all evil counsellors, in the name of Jesus.

5. Every evil finger pointing at me, wither, in the name of Jesus.

6. Lord, lead me to the rock that is higher than me, in Jesus' name.

7. Any mountain that the enemy has constructed before me, receive the thunder of God, in the name of Jesus.

8. All masquerading problems, be unmasked, in the name of Jesus.

9. I command every evil imagination against me to fail, in Jesus' name.

10
PRAYER WARFARE

Power Against Dream Criminals

Prayer is a gift to you and a privilege. The gift is offered to all and all may become the wielders of the great power in prayer. However, the fact remains that the power of prayer is least exercised by the average believer. You will do well to learn the art of warfare prayer. The present temperature of the prayer of many Christians needs to rise if they expect serious breakthroughs.

The prayer points in this book are targeted at certain needs so that as you are praying you will not be beating the air. This is how to go use the book:

Locate your area of need by looking at the table of contents.

Select appropriate scriptures promising you what you desire. Meditate on them and let them sink into your spirit.

Go about the prayers in any of the following ways as led by the Holy Spirit:

   a. Three days' night vigil, i.e praying from 10 P.M. to 5 A.M. three consecutive nights.

   b. Three days' fast (breaking daily), i.e. praying at intervals and breaking the fast at 6.00 P.M. or 9.00.P.M. daily.

   c. Seven days' night vigil, i.e. praying from 10 P.M. to 5 A.M. seven consecutive nights.

Power Against Dream Criminals

d. Seven days' fast (breaking daily), i.e. praying at intervals and breaking the fast at 6.00 P.M. or 9.00.P.M. daily.

e. Three or more days of dry fast. i.e., praying and fasting three or more days without any food or drink.

Pray aggressively.

NOTE: Spend part of vigil or fasting praying in the Spirit - Praying in the Spirit is an ability to pray in tongues as given utterance by the Holy Spirit. To pray in the Spirit, you must have been baptised in the Holy Ghost (not water baptism) - 1 Cor. 14:15.

You will be victorious in Jesus' name.

DREAM CRIMINALS MUST DIE

Confession

Isaiah 49:26: And I will feed them that oppress thee with their own flesh; and they shall be drunken with their own blood, as with sweet wine: and all flesh shall know that I the LORD *am* thy Saviour and thy Redeemer, the mighty One of Jacob.

Praise Worship

1. Lord, show me dreams, visions and restlessness that would advance my cause.

2. Let all satanic designs of oppression against me in dreams and visions be frustrated, in the name of Jesus.

3. Let all the enemies of my good dreams and visions on my home be rendered impotent, in the name of Jesus.

4. I bind the activities of demonic manipulation in dreams and visions, in the name of Jesus.

5. I stand against dream defeats, in the name of Jesus.

6. I claim freedom from satanic and restless dreams, in the name of Jesus.

7. Let all satanic designs of oppression against me in dreams and visions be frustrated, in the name of Jesus.

8. I claim all the good things which God has revealed to me through dreams. I reject all bad and satanic dreams, in the name of Jesus.

Power Against Dream Criminals

9. (You are going to be specific here. Place your hand on your chest and talk to God specifically about the dreams which need to be cancelled. Cancel it with all your strength. If it needs fire, command the fire of God to burn it to ashes.)

10. O Lord, perform the necessary surgical operation in my life and change all that had gone wrong in the spirit world.

11. I claim back all the good things which I have lost as a result of defeat and attacks in my dreams, in the name of Jesus.

12. I arrest every spiritual attacker and paralyse their activities in my life, in the name of Jesus.

13. I retrieve my stolen virtues, goodness and blessings, in Jesus' name.

14. Let all satanic manipulations through dreams be dissolved, in the name of Jesus.

15. Let all arrows, gunshots, wounds, harassment, opposition in dreams return to the senders, in the name of Jesus.

16. I reject every evil spiritual load placed on me through dreams, in the name of Jesus.

17. All spiritual animals (cats, dogs, snakes, crocodiles) paraded against me, be chained and returned to the senders, in the name of Jesus.

18. Holy Ghost, purge my intestine and my blood from satanic foods and injections.

19. I break every evil covenant and initiation through dreams, in the name of Jesus.

Power Against Dream Criminals

20. I disband all the hosts of darkness set against me, in the name of Jesus.
21. Every evil imagination and plan contrary to my life, fail woefully, in the name of Jesus.
22. Every doorway and ladder to satanic invasion in my life, be abolished forever by the blood of Jesus.
23. I loose myself from curses, hexes, spells, bewitchment and evil domination directed against me through dreams, in the name of Jesus.
24. I command you ungodly powers to release me, in the name of Jesus.
25. Let all past satanic defeats in the dream, be converted to victory, in the name of Jesus.
26. Let all tests in the dream be converted to testimonies, in Jesus' name.
27. Let all trials in the dream be converted to triumphs, in Jesus' name.
28. Let all failures in the dream be converted to success, in Jesus' name.
29. Let all scars in the dream be converted to stars, in Jesus' name.
30. Let all bondage in the dream be converted to freedom, in Jesus' name.
31. Let all losses in the dream be converted to gains, in Jesus' name.

Power Against Dream Criminals

32. Let all oppositions in the dream be converted to victory, in Jesus' name.

33. Let all weaknesses in the dream be converted to strength, in the name of Jesus.

34. Let all negative in the dream be converted to positive, in Jesus' name.

35. I release myself from every infirmity introduced into my life through dreams, in the name of Jesus.

36. Let all attempts by the enemy to deceive me through dreams fail woefully, in the name of Jesus.

37. I reject evil spiritual husband, wife, children, marriage, engagement, trading, pursuit, ornament, money, friend, relative, etc. in Jesus' name.

38. Lord Jesus, wash my spiritual eyes, ears and mouth with Your blood.

39. The God who answereth by fire, answer by fire whenever any spiritual attacker comes against me, in the name of Jesus.

40. Lord Jesus, replace all satanic dreams with heavenly visions and divinely-inspired dreams.

41. Confess these scriptures out loud: Psalm :1-, 1Cor. 1:1, Psalm 1

42. I command every evil plantation in my life, **come out with all your roots in the name of Jesus!** *(Lay your hands on your stomach and keep repeating the emphasized area.)*

Power Against Dream Criminals

43. Evil strangers in my body, come all the way out of your hiding places, in the name of Jesus.

44. I disconnect any conscious or unconscious linkage with demonic caterers, in the name of Jesus.

45. Let all avenues of eating or drinking spiritual poisons in the dreams be closed, in the name of Jesus.

46. I cough out and vomit any food eaten from the table of the devil, in the name of Jesus. (*Cough them out and vomit them in faith. Prime the expulsion*).

47. Let all negative materials circulating in my blood stream be evacuated, in the name of Jesus.

48. I drink the blood of Jesus. (*Physically swallow and drink it in faith. Keep doing this for some time*).

49. Let all evil spiritual feeders warring against me drink their own blood and eat their own flesh.

50. I command all demonic food utensils fashioned against me to be roasted, in the name of Jesus.

51. Holy Ghost fire, circulate all over my body.

52. I command all physical poisons inside my system to be neutralized, in the name of Jesus.

53. Let all evil assignments fashioned against me through the mouth gate be nullified, in the name of Jesus.

54. Let all spiritual problems attached to any hour of the night be cancelled, in the name of Jesus. (*Pick the periods from midnight down to : a.m.*).

Power Against Dream Criminals

55. Bread of heaven, fill me till I want no more.

56. Let all catering equipments of evil caterers attached to me be destroyed, in the name of Jesus.

57. I command my digestive system to reject every evil command, in the name of Jesus.

58. Let all satanic designs of oppression against me in dreams and visions be frustrated, in the name of Jesus.

59. I remove my name from the register of evil feeders with the blood of Jesus.

60. Let the habitation of evil caterers become desolate, in Jesus' name.

61. I paralyse the spirit that brings bad dreams to me, in the name of Jesus.

62. Let the fire of the Holy Ghost destroy any evil list containing my name, in the name of Jesus.

63. Let the fire of the Holy Ghost destroy any of my picture in the air, land and sea, in the name of Jesus.

64. I destroy any coffin prepared for me, in the name of Jesus.

65. I cancel and wipe off all evil dreams, in the name of Jesus.

66. I destroy every satanic accident organised for my sake, in Jesus' name.

67. I render all evil night creatures powerless, in the name of Jesus.

68. Let the blood of Jesus wash all the organs in my body, in Jesus' name.

Power Against Dream Criminals

69. Let all sicknesses planted in my life throw evil spiritual food be destroyed, in the name of Jesus.

70. Let the blood of Jesus erase all evil dreams, in the name of Jesus.

71. Let the fire of God boil all rivers harbouring demons, in Jesus' name.

72. Let all evil dreams be replaced with blessings, in the name of Jesus.

73. I command all my good dreams to come to pass, in the name of Jesus.

74. I release myself from every dream pollution, in the name of Jesus.

75. Let every satanic attack against my life in my dreams be converted to victory, in the name of Jesus.

76. Let all rivers, trees, forests, evil companions, evil pursuers, visions of dead relatives, snakes, spirit husbands, spirit wives, and masquerades manipulated against me in the dream be completely destroyed by the power in the blood of the Lord Jesus.

77. Every power and spirit in the likeness of snakes attacking me in my dreams, be buried, in the name of Jesus.

78. Let every demonic influence targeted at destroying my vision, dream and ministry receive total disappointment, in the name of Jesus.

79. O Lord, enlarge my coasts beyond my wildest dream.

Power Against Dream Criminals

80. I stand against every dream of defeat, in the name of Jesus.

81. I send the arrows or any gun shot in the dream back to the senders, in the name of Jesus.

82. I paralyse all the night caterers and I forbid their food in my dream, in the name of Jesus.

83. Let all the contamination in my life through dreams be cleansed by the blood of Jesus.

84. I cancel all visions, dreams, words, curses contrary to my progress, in the name of Jesus.

85. I bind every demon that pollutes spiritual vision and dreams, in the name of Jesus.

86. Divine revelations, spiritual visions, dreams and information will not become scarce commodities in my life, in the name of Jesus.

87. Every satanic animal in the dream, fall down and die, in Jesus' name.

88. Let all the enemies of my good dreams and visions concerning my home be rendered impotent, in the name of Jesus.

89. My imagination and dreams will not be used against me, in Jesus' name.

90. By the blood of Jesus, I rebuke every attacking and fearful dreams, in the name of Jesus.

91. Let the evil vision and dream on my life evaporate from the camp of the enemy, in the name of Jesus.

Power Against Dream Criminals

92. Every cause of demotion in the dream in my life, be nullified by the blood of Jesus.

93. Every cause of confused and unprogressive dreams in my life, be nullified by the blood of Jesus.

94. Every cause of being harassed in the dreams by familiar faces in my life, be nullified by the blood of Jesus.

95. My dream will not become a nightmare, in the name of Jesus.

96. Any anti-progress materials fired into my life through dreams, be nullified, in the name of Jesus.

97. By the blood of Jesus, I nullify every dream of . . . (pick from the under listed).

 - swimming in the water
 - eating strange food
 - drinking coke and fanta
 - having sex with fair or dark women / men
 - running without getting to a stop
 - talking alone without response
 - getting married with dirty garment
 - having children or breast-feeding
 - having bald head or hair falling off
 - sitting on a broken or cracked fence
 - falling inside the mud
 - eating inside a broken plate

Power Against Dream Criminals

- getting married without wedding suit/dress
- sleeping/playing in an uncompleted building

98. Every witchcraft hand planting evil seeds in my life through dreams, wither and burn to ashes, in the name of Jesus.

99. Every marine witchcraft that has introduced spirit husband/wife or child in my dreams, be roasted by fire, in the name of Jesus.

100. Every agent of marine witchcraft posing as my husband, wife or child in my dreams, be roasted by fire, in the name of Jesus.

101. Every agent of marine witchcraft assigned to attack my finances through dreams, fall down and perish, in the name of Jesus.

102. Every power and spirit attacking me in the person of snakes in my dreams, be buried, in the name of Jesus.

103. I command all my properties captured by spiritual robbers in the dream to become too hot to handle and to come back to me, in the name of Jesus.

104. I bind every demon that pollutes spiritual vision and dreams, in the name of Jesus.

105. Wonderful Lord, I reverse any defeat that I have ever suffered in the dream, in the name of Jesus.

106. Any dream that I have dreamt that is good and for God, I receive it, and those that are satanic, I reject them, in the name of Jesus.

Power Against Dream Criminals

107. Every night and dream attacks and its consequences, be nullified, in the name of Jesus.
108. I claim freedom from satanic and restless dreams, in Jesus' name.
109. I claim freedom from importing anxiety and shameful thoughts into my dream, in the name of Jesus.
110. I stand against dream defeats and its effects, in the name of Jesus.
111. Let all satanic designs of oppression against me in dreams and visions be frustrated, in the name of Jesus.
112. Let the evil vision and dream on my life evaporate and condense in the camp of the enemy, in the name of Jesus.
113. Every dream of demotions to junior school, be dismantled. I shall go from glory to glory, in the name of Jesus.
114. By the power in the blood of Jesus, I cancel the maturity dates of any evil dreams with my life.
115. You God of promotion, promote me beyond my widest dreams, in the name of Jesus.
116. Every sickness planted in the dream into my life, get out now and go back to your sender, in the name of Jesus.
117. Let life be squeezed out of my dream attackers, in Jesus' name.
118. By the power in the blood of Jesus, I command all my buried good dreams and visions to be exhumed.

Power Against Dream Criminals

119. By the power in the blood of Jesus, I command all my polluted good dreams and visions to receive divine solution.

120. By the power in the blood of Jesus, I command all dream and vision killers that are working against the manifestation of my good dreams and visions to be paralysed.

121. By the power in the blood of Jesus, I command every good dream and vision that has been stolen away to be restored with fresh fire.

122. By the power in the blood of Jesus, I command every good dream and vision that has been transferred to be restored with fresh fire.

123. By the power in the blood of Jesus, I command every good dream and vision that has been poisoned to be neutralised.

124. By the power in the blood of Jesus, I command every good dream and vision that has been amputated to receive divine strength.

125. Let all the contamination in my life through dreams be cleansed by the blood of Jesus.

126. Any anti-progress material fired into my life through dreams, be nullified, in the name of Jesus.

127. I resist the threat of death in my dream by fire, in Jesus' name.

Power Against Dream Criminals

128. Every evil dream that other people have had about me, I cancel them in the astral world, in the name of Jesus.

129. Every image of satan in my dream, I curse you to wither now, in the name of Jesus.

130. I command every dream of demotion to stop, in Jesus' name.

131. Every arrow of death in the dream, come out and go back to your sender, in the name of Jesus.

132. Every sponsored dream of poverty by household wickedness against my life, vanish, in the name of Jesus.

133. I dash every poverty dream to the ground, in the name of Jesus.

134. I cancel the manipulation of every satanic dream, in Jesus' name.

135. You powers of the night polluting my night dreams, be paralysed, in the name of Jesus.

136. Every anti-prosperity dream, die, in the mighty name of Jesus.

137. Let all satanic designs of oppression against me in dreams and visions be frustrated, in Jesus' name.

138. I paralyse the spirits that bring bad dreams to me, in Jesus' name.

139. I cancel and wipe off all evil dreams, in the name of Jesus.

140. Let the blood of Jesus erase all evil dreams in my life, in Jesus' name.

Power Against Dream Criminals

141. My dreams, my joys, my breakthroughs, that have been buried in the dark world, be reversed now, in the name of Jesus.

142. Every dreaming serpent, go back to your sender, in Jesus' name.

143. Every power planting affliction into my life in the dream, be buried alive, in the name of Jesus.

144. Any evil programme, programmed into my life from my dream, be dismantled now, in the name of Jesus.

145. O Lord, deliver me from witchcraft dreams.

146. Satanic dreams, go back to your senders, in the name of Jesus.

147. I reject oppression, I claim liberty, in the name of Jesus.

148. I reject infirmity, I claim divine health, in the name of Jesus.

149. I reject curses, I claim God's blessing, in the name of Jesus.

150. I reject poverty, I claim wealth, in the name of Jesus.

151. I reject turbulence, I claim the peace of God, in the name of Jesus.

152. I reject tragedy, I claim goodness, in the name of Jesus.

153. I reject satanic dreams, I claim divine revelations, in Jesus' name.

154. I reject failure, I claim good prospects, in the name of Jesus.

Power Against Dream Criminals

155. I reject frustration, I claim multiple promotions, in the name of Jesus.

156. You powers of the night polluting my night dreams, be paralysed, in the name of Jesus.

157. Every sponsored dream of poverty, by household wickedness against my life, vanish, in the name of Jesus.

158. I drink the blood of Jesus to neutralize every satanic food or drink taken in the dream, in the name of Jesus.

159. I cancel every evil dream by the blood of Jesus and the fire of the Holy Ghost, in the name of Jesus.

160. Every instrument of satanic retaliation, die in the name of Jesus.

161. Every entrance of satanic influence on my life, die in Jesus' name.

162. O Lord, kill every internal destiny killer.

163. Blood of Jesus, recover my stolen birthright, in the name of Jesus.

164. Every power of familiar spirit on my destiny die, in the name of Jesus.

165. I shall fulfil my divine agenda, in the name of Jesus.

166. O Lord, stir the Holy Ghost in my spirit, in the name of Jesus.

167. Every anti-testimony altar, die in the name of Jesus.

168. Every power that wants me to attend MFM in vain, die, in Jesus' name

Power Against Dream Criminals

169. Stubborn witchcraft, I rub your pepper of affliction on your body, in the name of Jesus.

170. Amputators and emptiers, loose your hold upon my life and die, in the name of Jesus.

171. Evil birds assigned against my mounting up, crash-land and die, in the name of Jesus.

172. Every bat/vulture/dog programmed into my dream, die, in the name of Jesus.

173. None shall pluck my stars out of my hands, in the name of Jesus.

174. None shall pluck my stars out of my head, in the name of Jesus.

175. My Glory shall not sink, in the name of Jesus.

176. Every friendly Judas in my life, be exposed and disgraced, in the name of Jesus.

177. Evil hands pointed against me, dry up, in the name of Jesus.

178. By the power that divided the Red Sea let my problem die, in the name of Jesus.

179. Every river in my place of birth, release my virtue, in Jesus' name.

180. I sack every satanic checkpoint mounted against my success, in the name of Jesus.

181. Let deliverance take place in my dream, in the name of Jesus.

Power Against Dream Criminals

182. O Lord, find the dragon in my life and kill it, in the name of Jesus.

183. Every foundation of witchcraft in my family, be dismantled, in the name of Jesus.

184. O God, attack my ignorance, my lack, and my mountains, in the name of Jesus.

185. By the power that sank Pharaoh, by the power that disgraced Goliath, by sus.

186. O God, attack my ignorance, my lack, and my mountains, in the name of Jesus.

187. By the power that sank Pharaoh, by the power that disgraced Goliath, by the power that command worms on Herod, let my stubborn problems die, in the name of Jesus.

188. Every power cursing my destiny, die, in the name of Jesus.

189. You my full time enemies, I strike you with chaos and confusion, in the name of Jesus.

190. Every witchcraft incantation against my destiny, die, in Jesus' name.

191. I go back to Adam and Eve on both sides of my generation and I cut off every evil root, in the name of Jesus.

192. Every wicked assignment spirit assigned against my destiny, fail and fall by fire, in the name of Jesus.

Power Against Dream Criminals

193. Bitter water flow out of my life by fire, in the name of Jesus.
194. Every evil tooth biting my goodness, be dashed to pieces, in the name of Jesus.
195. No contrary spirit within my family shall have peace, in Jesus' name.
196. Every satanic crowd gathered to mock me, be disgraced, in the name of Jesus.
197. I break every covenant that strengthens the enemy, in Jesus' name.
198. My enemies shall become stepping stones to my higher ground, in the name of Jesus.
199. Evil mountains, get out of my situation, in the name of Jesus.
200. My cry, provoke angelic violence, in the name of Jesus.
201. O Lord, do everything in Your power to bring my victory.
202. Any pot calling my name for destruction, scatter, in the name of Jesus.
203. Every foundational barrier to greatness, die, in the name of Jesus.
204. Every fountain of poverty, break, in the name of Jesus.
205. Every serpent and scorpion working against my destiny, dry up and die, in the name of Jesus.
206. You foundation of wickedness, be uprooted, in the name of Jesus.

Power Against Dream Criminals

207. Every evil magnet within me, roast, in the name of Jesus.
208. I separate my life from every witchcraft programme, in Jesus' name.
209. Every witchcraft battle at the edge of my breakthroughs, die, in the name of Jesus.
210. Every power causing warfare at the edge of my breakthrough, carry away your warfare, in the name of Jesus.
211. Every familiar spirit operating at the edge of my breakthrough, die, in the name of Jesus.
212. O Lord, to You and to You alone be all the glory for the assurance that You have answered all my prayers.

Power Against Dream Criminals

HOLY SPIRIT, FILL ME AFRESH

Confession

Acts 1:8: But ye shall receive power, after that the Holy Ghost is come upon you: and ye shall be witnesses unto me both in Jerusalem, and in all Judaea, and in Samaria, and unto the uttermost part of the earth.

Praise Worship

1. Oh Lord, make me Your rod to break water spirits into pieces, in the name of Jesus.
2. Let the blood of Jesus erase every evil record fashioned against me, in the name of Jesus.
3. Let every evil rope on my loins be broken, in Jesus' name.
4. I come against marine spirits by the Word of the Lord, in the name of Jesus.
5. I dispose you of all your marine certificates, in the name of Jesus.
6. I command you to release all my good things you are holding in bondage, in the name of Jesus.
7. I pronounce jubilee upon my life, in the name of Jesus.
8. I dismantle and frustrate every satanic investment, in the name of Jesus.
9. O Lord, increase my strength for battle.
10. I ride on the horses of war, in the name of Jesus.

Power Against Dream Criminals

11. Let the arrow of the Lord be strong in the heart of my enemies, in the name of Jesus.
12. I arrest the horses, chariots and the horsemen, in the name of Jesus.
13. I frustrate their token, in the name of Jesus.
14. I make their diviners mad, in the name of Jesus.
15. O Lord, make me Your sword.
16. O Lord, make me Your rod.
17. O Lord, make me a vehicle of deliverance.
18. I come by faith to mount Zion, Lord, command deliverance upon my life.
19. O Lord, water me from the waters of God.
20. Let the careful siege of the enemy be dismantled, in the name of Jesus.
21. O Lord, defend Your interest in my life.
22. Everything written in the cycle of the moon, be blotted out, in the name of Jesus.
23. Everything programmed into the sun, moon and stars against my life, be dismantled, in the name of Jesus.
24. Every evil thing programmed into my genes, be dismantled, in the name of Jesus.
25. I shake out seasons of failure and frustrations from my life, in the name of Jesus.

Power Against Dream Criminals

26. I overthrow every wicked law programmed against my life, in the name of Jesus.

27. I ordain a new time and season and profitable law for my life, in the name of Jesus.

28. I speak unto the palaces of the queen of the coast and of the rivers, in the name of Jesus.

29. I speak unto the altars speaking against the purpose of God for my life, in the name of Jesus.

30. I declare myself a virgin for the Lord, in Jesus' name.

31. Let every evil veil upon my life tear to pieces, in the name of Jesus.

32. Every wall between me and the visitation of God, be broken, in the name of Jesus.

33. Let the counsel of God prosper in my life, in the name of Jesus.

34. I destroy the power of any demonic seed in my life from the womb, in the name of Jesus.

35. I speak unto my umbilical gate to overthrow all negative parental spirits, in the name of Jesus.

36. O Lord, let Your time of refreshing come upon me from the presence of the Lord.

Power Against Dream Criminals

DEALING WITH MARINE ATTACKS AGAINST DESTINY

Confession

Col. 1:13-17: Who hath delivered us from the power of darkness, and hath translated *us* into the kingdom of his dear Son: ¹⁴In whom we have redemption through his blood, *even* the forgiveness of sins: ¹⁵Who is the image of the invisible God, the firstborn of every creature: ¹⁶For by him were all things created, that are in heaven, and that are in earth, visible and invisible, whether *they be* thrones, or dominions, or principalities, or powers: all things were created by him, and for him: ¹⁷And he is before all things, and by him all things consist.

Praise Worship

1. I address any evil river from my place of birth, in the name of Jesus.
2. Let the armoury of the Lord be opened unto me, in the name of Jesus.
3. I refuse and reject ancestral covenant with water spirits, in the name of Jesus.
4. I bring the hook of the Lord over every water spirit working against my life, in the name of Jesus.
5. I bring the rebuke of the Lord upon every marine spirit working against my life, in the name of Jesus.

Power Against Dream Criminals

6. I anchor the heads of water spirits to divine judgement, in the name of Jesus.

7. Every deposit of marine spirit, be flushed out by the blood of Jesus.

8. Every deposit of water spirit, be flushed out by the blood of Jesus.

9. I break every dedication to water spirits, in Jesus' name.

10. Any blood and water pollution of my body come out by fire, in the name of Jesus.

11. I destroy every record of my name and destiny in the marine world, in the name of Jesus.

12. I redeem myself by the blood of Jesus from every sex trap, in the name of Jesus.

13. I erase the engraving of my name on any evil marriage record, in the name of Jesus.

14. I reject and renounce every evil spiritual marriage, in the name of Jesus.

15. Jesus is my original spouse and is jealous over me.

16. I issue a bill of divorcement for every spirit wife/husband, in the name of Jesus.

17. I bind every spirit wife/husband with everlasting chains, in the name of Jesus.

18. Let heavenly testimony overcome every evil testimony of hell, in the name of Jesus.

Power Against Dream Criminals

19. O Lord, bring to my remembrance every spiritual trap and contracts.
20. Let the blood of Jesus purge me of every contaminating materials, in the name of Jesus.
21. Let the spirit husband/wife fall down and die, in the name of Jesus.
22. Let all their children attached to me fall down and die, in the name of Jesus.
23. I burn your certificates and destroy your rings, in the name of Jesus.
24. I execute judgement against water spirits and I declare that you are reserved against everlasting chains in darkness, in the name of Jesus.
25. O Lord, contend with those who are contending with me.
26. I announce to the heavens that I am forever married to Jesus, in the name of Jesus.
27. Every trademark of water spirit, be shaken out of my life, in the name of Jesus.
28. Every evil writing engraved by iron pen, be wiped off by the blood of Jesus.
29. I bring the blood of Jesus over the spirit that does not want to go, in the name of Jesus.
30. I bring the blood of Jesus over every evidence that can be tendered by wicked spirits against me, in the name of Jesus.

Power Against Dream Criminals

31. I file a counter-report in heaven against water spirits, in the name of Jesus.
32. I refuse to bury any evidence that the enemy may use against me, in the name of Jesus.
33. Let satanic exhibition be destroyed by the blood of Jesus.
34. According to the word of God in Isaiah chapter 54, verse 5, I declare that there is no vacancy for spirit wife/husband in my life, in the name of Jesus.
35. O Lord, cleanse all the soiled parts of my life.
36. O Lord, refresh every dry area of my life.
37. O Lord, heal every wounded part of my life.
38. O Lord, bend every evil that has become rigid in my life.
39. O Lord, re-align every satanic straying in my life.
40. O Lord, let the fire of the Holy Spirit warm every satanic frozen area in my life.
41. O Lord, give me a life that kills death.
42. O Lord, kindle in me the fire of charity.
43. O Lord, glue me together where I am opposed to myself.
44. O Lord, enrich me with Your gifts.
45. O Lord, quicken me and increase my desire of the things of heaven.
46. By Your rulership, O Lord, let the lust of the flesh in my life die.
47. Lord Jesus, increase daily in my life.

Power Against Dream Criminals

48. Lord Jesus, maintain Your gifts in my life.
49. O Lord, refine and purge my life by Your fire.
50. Holy Spirit, inflame and fire my heart, in Jesus' name.
51. Lord Jesus, lay Your hands upon me and quench every rebellion in me.
52. Holy Ghost fire, begin to burn away every self-centredness in me, in the name of Jesus.
53. Father Lord, breathe Your life-giving breath into my soul, in the name of Jesus.
54. O Lord, make me ready to go wherever You send me.
55. Lord Jesus, never let me shut You out.
56. Lord Jesus, never let me try to limit You to my capacity.
57. Lord Jesus, work freely in me and through me.
58. O Lord, purify the channels of my life.
59. Let Your heat O Lord, consume my will, in Jesus' name.
60. Let the flame of the Holy Spirit blaze upon the altar of my heart, in the name of Jesus.
61. Lord Jesus, come like blood into my veins.
62. O Lord, order my spirit and fashion my life in Your will.
63. Let Your fire burn out all that is not holy in my life, in the name of Jesus.
64. O Lord, let Your fire generate power in my life, in the name of Jesus.

Power Against Dream Criminals

65. Lord Jesus, impart unto me thoughts higher than my own thoughts.

66. Holy Spirit, come as dew and refresh me, in Jesus' name.

67. Holy Spirit, guide me in the way of liberty, in the name of Jesus.

68. Holy Spirit, blow upon me such that sin would no more find place in me, in the name of Jesus.

69. Holy Spirit, where my love is cold, warm me, in the name of Jesus.

70. Thank God for His mighty presence upon your life.

Power Against Dream Criminals

DESTROYING WITCHCRAFT ATTACKS AGAINST DESTINY

Confession

In the name of Jesus, I believe the word of God is steadfast and unshakeable, endures forever, powerful and it is the power of God that is able to deliver me out of any bondage.

The word of God is God Himself speaking and not man. Therefore, nothing shall be impossible for me because of the word of God I believe in my heart and confess with my mouth.

Father Lord, as I make this confession now, I pray that You will watch over Your word to perform it, because You are a faithful God. You are not a man that You should lie, neither the son of man that You should repent. Rather You will not break Your covenant, nor alter the word which has gone forth out of Your mouth.

It is written, when I ask, I should believe and receive. As I make this confession and go into prayer, I will receive, according to the word of God, dominion and power, because I know God will prove Himself strong on my behalf, for my heart is focused on Him.

I know who I am in Christ. I have been purchased by the blood of Jesus Christ that was shed for me on the cross of calvary. I am a child of God. I am called by the name of the Lord. I am bought by the blood of the Lamb of God. I believe the power in the blood of Jesus. Jesus has translated my life from the kingdom of darkness into His own marvelous kingdom of light and peace. I now belong to the kingdom of God. I have the keys of the kingdom of God in my hands to bind and to loose. I have the authority to trample under my feet, serpents, scorpions and all the power of the enemy.

Power Against Dream Criminals

Jesus Christ, through His death, has destroyed satan, who had the power of death. Jesus has delivered my life from death and damnation. Before Jesus ascended, He first of all descended into the lower parts of the earth and stripped the devil of all his power over me. Jesus has taken from satan the keys of death and hell and has given them to me to bind and to loose.

By virtue of the work Jesus Christ did on the cross, I have power over all the power of the enemy. He has wiped out all the handwriting of requirements that were against me, taking them out of the way, having nailed them to the cross. He disarmed principalities and powers and made a show of them openly, triumphing over them in it.

I hold in my hand now the victory won for me by my Saviour Jesus Christ on the cross of calvary and I say, "Be shattered Oh you witches and powers of wickedness and be broken in pieces. Give ear all you powers of wickedness from my place of birth or origin, gird yourselves and you shall be broken in pieces. Take your counsel together and it will come to nothing. Chant your incantations, they will not stand, for the Lord is with me as a mighty and terrible one. Therefore, you shall stumble and fall."

"Encamp against me, but my heart shall not fear, for in the name of the Lord, I will destroy you. The Lord is the strength of my life, of whom shall I be afraid. Surround me like bees and I will quench you all, like a fire of thorns."

"Fashion your weapons of wickedness, and they will not prosper. Rise up against me in judgement with all your legal grounds and you shall all be condemned because that is my heritage as a servant of God."

"I shall not die but live. Any power that has ever led me captive shall go into captivity. They that afflict and oppress me shall be

Power Against Dream Criminals

ashamed. God will contend with all who contend with me. He will feed those who oppress me with their own flesh and they shall be drunken with their own blood as with sweet wine, for the Lord will bring upon them the day of the doom and destroy them with double destruction."

It is written that God will light my lamp and enlighten my darkness. But every satanic agent or power oppressing me shall grope in the day time as in thick blackness and darkness.

It is written that I should be strong in the Lord and in the power of His might, therefore I ask that as I go into prayer right now the Lord will be my strength; strength to run through a troop, to leap over any wall, to pursue and overtake my enemies, to recover my stolen properties, to beat them small as the dust, to withstand and overcome all spiritual oppositions and distractions.

I hold in my hand the shield of faith for it is written that whosoever is born of God overcometh the world. And this is the victory that overcometh the world and its wickedness, even my faith.

In faith I go into this prayer session. In faith I have the victory. In faith my enemies are all subdued under my feet and none shall be able to escape.

My heart steadfastly believes the word of God. I have confessed with my mouth and by the word of my mouth let me be justified Oh Lord and let all my enemies be condemned. I seal my confession with the blood of Jesus. (Amen.)

Praise Worship

1. Let the thunder of God locate and dismantle the throne of witchcraft in my household, in the name of Jesus.

Power Against Dream Criminals

2. Let every seat of witchcraft in my household be roasted with the fire of God, in the name of Jesus.

3. Let the altar of witchcraft in my household be roasted, in the name of Jesus.

4. Let the thunder of God scatter beyond redemption the foundation of witchcraft in my household, in Jesus' name.

5. Every stronghold or refuge of my household witches, be destroyed, in the name of Jesus.

6. Every hiding place and secret place of witchcraft in my family, be exposed by fire, in the name of Jesus.

7. Let every local and international witchcraft network of my household witches be shattered to pieces, in Jesus' name.

8. Let the communication system of my household witches be frustrated, in the name of Jesus.

9. Let the terrible fire of God consume the transportation of my household witchcraft, in the name of Jesus.

10. Every agent ministering at the altar of witchcraft in my household, fall down and die, in the name of Jesus.

11. Let the thunder and the fire of God locate the storehouses and strongrooms of my household witchcraft harbouring my blessings and pull them down, in the name of Jesus.

12. Let any witchcraft curse working against me be revoked by the blood of Jesus.

13. Every decision, vow and covenant of household witchcraft affecting me, be nullified by the blood of Jesus.

Power Against Dream Criminals

14. I destroy with the fire of God, every weapon of witchcraft used against me, in the name of Jesus.
15. Any material taken from my body and placed on witchcraft altar, be roasted by the fire of God, in the name of Jesus.
16. I reverse every witchcraft burial fashioned against me, in the name of Jesus.
17. Every trap set for me by witches begin to catch your owners, in the name of Jesus.
18. Every witchcraft padlock fashioned against any area of my life be roasted, in the name of Jesus.
19. Let the wisdom of my household witches be converted to foolishness, in the name of Jesus.
20. Let the wickedness of my household enemies overturn them, in the name of Jesus.
21. I deliver my soul from every witchcraft bewitchment, in the name of Jesus.
22. Any witchcraft bird flying for my sake, fall down and die and be roasted to ashes, in the name of Jesus.
23. Any of my blessing traded out by household witches be returned to me, in the name of Jesus.
24. Any of my blessings and testimonies swallowed by witches, be converted to hot coals of fire of God and be vomited, in the name of Jesus.
25. I break myself loose from every bondage of witchcraft covenant, in the name of Jesus.

Power Against Dream Criminals

26. Any witchcraft coven where any of my blessings are hidden, be roasted by the fire of God, in Jesus' name.

27. (Lay your right hand on your head) Every witchcraft spirit plantation, pollution, deposits and materials in my body be melted by the fire of God and be flushed out by the blood of Jesus.

28. Every evil ever done to me through witchcraft attack, be reversed, in the name of Jesus.

29. Every damage done to my destiny through witchcraft operations, be reversed now, in the name of Jesus.

30. Every witchcraft hand planting evil seeds in my life through dream attacks, wither and burn to ashes, in the name of Jesus.

31. Every witchcraft obstacle and hindrance put on the road to my desired miracle and success, be removed by the East wind of God, in the name of Jesus.

32. Every witchcraft chants, spells and projections made against me, I bind you and turn you against your owner, in the name of Jesus.

33. I frustrate every plot, device, scheme and projects of witchcraft designed to affect any area of my life, in the name of Jesus.

34. Any witch projecting into the blood of any animal in order to do me harm or evil, be trapped in the body of such an animal forever, in the name of Jesus.

Power Against Dream Criminals

35. Any drop of my blood sucked by any witch, be vomited now, in the name of Jesus.

36. Any part of me shared out amongst household / village witches, I recover you, in the name of Jesus.

37. Any organ of my body that has been exchanged for another one through witchcraft operations, be replaced now, in the name of Jesus.

38. I recover any of my virtues / blessings shared out amongst village / household witches, in Jesus' name.

39. I reverse the evil effect of any witchcraft invocation or summoning of my spirit, in the name of Jesus.

40. I loose my hands and feet from any witchcraft bewitchment and bondage, in the name of Jesus.

41. Let the blood of Jesus wash away every witchcraft identification mark on me or on any of my property, in Jesus' name.

42. I forbid any re-union or re-gathering of household and village witches against my life, in the name of Jesus.

43. Let the entire body system of my household witches be upset until they confess all their wickedness, in the name of Jesus.

As regards the household witches that are contrary to me:

44. Let the mercies of God be withdrawn from them, in Jesus' name.

Power Against Dream Criminals

45. Let them begin to grope in the daytime as in the thickness of a dark night, in the name of Jesus.

46. Let everything that has every worked for them begin to work against them, in the name of Jesus.

47. Let them not have a clothe to cover their shame, in Jesus' name.

48. Let as many of them as are stubbornly unrepentant be smitten by the sun in the day and by the moon at night, in the name of Jesus.

49. Let each step they take lead them to greater destruction, in the name of Jesus.

50. But as for me, let me dwell in the hollow of God's hand, in the name of Jesus.

51. Let the goodness and mercies of God now overwhelm me, in the name of Jesus.

52. I force feed witchcraft powers with their own blood, in the name of Jesus.

53. Every foundation of witchcraft in my household, be smashed by the Rock of ages, in the name of Jesus.

54. Every seat of witchcraft, receive the thunder fire of God, in the name of Jesus.

55. Every habitation of witchcraft, be scattered unto desolation, in the name of Jesus.

56. Every throne of witchcraft, be dismantled by fire, in the name of Jesus.

Power Against Dream Criminals

57. Every stronghold of witchcraft in my life, receive divine acid, in the name of Jesus.
58. Let the witchcraft network be shattered to pieces, in the name of Jesus.
59. Let their communication system be damaged by fire, in the name of Jesus.
60. Every stubborn and unrepentant witchcraft, be exposed and disgraced, in the name of Jesus.
61. Let their hiding place be dissolved by fire, in Jesus' name.
62. Let their transportation system scattered to pieces, in the name of Jesus.
63. I withdraw my blessings from every witchcraft storehouse and strongroom, in the name of Jesus.
64. Let every witchcraft curse go back to the sender seven fold, in the name of Jesus.
65. Every covenant of witchcraft, be melted by the blood of Jesus.
66. Every weapon of witchcraft, turn against your users, in the name of Jesus.
67. I reverse every witchcraft burial fashioned against me, in the name of Jesus.
68. I withdraw every organ of my body from any witchcraft altar, in the name of Jesus.
69. Every trap of witchcraft, catch your owners, in the name of Jesus.

Power Against Dream Criminals

70. Every witchcraft padlock fashioned against me, be roasted, in the name of Jesus.

71. I deliver my soul from every witchcraft bewitchment, in the name of Jesus.

72. Every damage done to my destiny by witchcraft, be reversed, in the name of Jesus.

73. Every witchcraft utterance and projections made against me, be overthrown, in the name of Jesus.

74. Any drop of my blood sucked by any witch, be vomitted now, in the name of Jesus.

75. I reverse the effect of every witchcraft summoning of my spirit, in the name of Jesus.

76. Every witchcraft identification mark, be wiped off by the blood of Jesus.

77. I frustrate every witchcraft exchange of my virtues, in the name of Jesus.

78. Anything planted in my life by witchcraft, come out now, in the name of Jesus.

79. Let each step taken by witchcraft against me lead them to greater destruction, in the name of Jesus.

80. I declare my environment and my house no-flying zone for witchcraft birds, in the name of Jesus.

81. I cut off the roots of witchcraft in the water, in the name of Jesus.

Power Against Dream Criminals

82. Anything deposited in my life by marine witchcraft, come out now, in the name of Jesus.

83. Anything deposited in my life by household witchcraft, come out now, in the name of Jesus.

84. Any serpent programmed into my body, come out by fire, in the name of Jesus.

85. O Lord, smite the power of Leviathan in my life, in the name of Jesus.

86. I cancel the poison of Leviathan in my life, in the name of Jesus.

87. Let the Lord reverse every law of Leviathan upon my life, in the name of Jesus.

88. I break the power of Leviathan over every department of my life, in the name of Jesus.

89. You Leviathan troubling my life, I put a sword in your heart and wound you now, in the name of Jesus.

90. Leviathan shall not guide my life, in the name of Jesus.

91. I put a hook in your jaw, in the name of Jesus and by the power in His blood.

92. Every serpentined area of my life, be cleared by the fire of God, in the name of Jesus.

93. Divine serpent eagle, eat up every serpent in my life, in the name of Jesus.

94. Every spiritual maggot inside my destiny, fall down and die, in Jesus' name.

Power Against Dream Criminals

95. Oh Lord, let Your divine purpose be settled in my life.

96. The devil will not break the back bone of my destiny, in the name of Jesus.

97. My destiny will not be put to shame, in Jesus' name.

98. My life will not disgrace Jesus, in the name of Jesus.

99. My name shall not disappear from the book of life, in the name of Jesus.

100. Every covenant of sorrow be broken now, in Jesus' name.

101. My angel will not disappear, in the name of Jesus.

102. My joy will not cease and my glory will not sink, in the name of Jesus.

103. All the gathering of the tormentors be disbanded, in the name of Jesus.

104. I capture all my floating blessings, in Jesus' name.

105. I prophesy on my destiny to move forward, in the name of Jesus.

106. Let the stones of my prayer locate my Goliath now, in the name of Jesus.

107. Any arrow of witchcraft fired into my life, gather yourselves together and go out, in the name of Jesus.

108. I remove myself from every witchcraft relocation by fire, in the name of Jesus.

109. I withdraw all my secrets from the possession of evil powers, in the name of Jesus.

Power Against Dream Criminals

110. Every witchcraft bird, vomit my blessings, in Jesus' name.

111. Place your right hand on your head as you go into this powerful session. Make sure that you are aggressive at this moment.

112. Make this powerful confession. Every effort of witchcraft to frustrate my work and my calling, I destroy you, in the name of Jesus. Father, increase my greatness and comfort me on every side. No household enemy shall be able to control my well-being any longer. All those who are looking down on me shall begin to look up to me. All those who are saying: "Let us see what Jesus will do for him". Oh Lord, surprise them. All those who are against me without any cause, let them go back and be brought into confusion, in the name of Jesus. Every door that witchcraft manipulation has closed against my progress, open, in the name of Jesus.

113. You, the strongman dedicated against me, fall down and die, in the name of Jesus.

114. The God that answereth by fire, answer me, in Jesus' name.

115. Let the stamp of heaven, stamp my prayer requests, in the name of Jesus.

116. Let every prayer point I prayed today become testimonies, in the name of Jesus.

Power Against Dream Criminals

1. Be Prepared
2. Breakthrough Prayers For Business Professionals
3. Brokenness
4. Born Great, But Tied Down
5. Can God Trust You?
6. Criminals In The House of God
7. Contending For The Kingdom
8. Dealing With Local Satanic Technology
9. Dealing With Witchcraft Barbers
10. Dealing With Hidden Curses
11. Dealing With The Evil Powers of Your Father's House
12. Dealing With Unprofitable Roots
13. Deliverance: God's Medicine Bottle
14. Deliverance By Fire
15. Deliverance From Spirit Husband And Spirit Wife
16. Deliverance of The Conscience
17. Deliverance of The Head
18. Destiny Clinic
19. Destroying The Evil Umbrella
20. Drawers of Power From The Heavenlies
21. Dominion Prosperity
22. Evil Appetite
23. Facing Both Ways
24. Family Deliverance

Power Against Dream Criminals

25. Fasting And Prayer
26. Failure In The School Of Prayer
27. Freedom From The Grip of Witchcraft
28. From Adversity To Testimony
29. For We Wrestle . . .
30. Holy Cry
31. Holy Fever
32. How To Obtain Personal Deliverance (Second Edition)
33. How To Pray When Surrounded By The Enemies
34. Idols Of The Heart
35. Is This What They Died For?
36. Limiting God
37. Meat For Champions
38. Overpowering Witchcraft
39. Paying The Evil Tithes
40. Personal Spiritual Check-up
41. Power Against Coffin Spirits
42. Power Against Destiny Criminals
43. Power Against Destiny Quenchers
44. Power Against Dream Criminals
45. Power Against Local Wickedness
46. Power Against Marine Spirits
47. Power Against Spiritual Terrorists
48. Power For Explosive Success

Power Against Dream Criminals

49. Power Must Change Hands
50. Pray Your Way To Breakthroughs (Third Edition)
51. Prayer Rain
52. Prayer is the Battle
53. Prayer Strategies For Spinsters And Bachelors
54. Prayers To Kill Enchantment and Divination
55. Prayers To Move From Minimum To Maximum
56. Prayer Warfare Against 70 Mad Spirits
57. Prayers To Destroy Diseases And Infirmities
58. Praying Against The Spirit of The Valley
59. Praying To Dismantle Witchcraft
60. Release From Destructive Covenants
61. Revoking Evil Decrees
62. Satanic Diversion Of The Black Race
63. Silencing The Birds of Darkness
64. Smite The Enemy And He Will Flee
65. Spiritual Warfare And The Home
66. Strategic Praying
67. Strategy Of Warfare Praying
68. Students In The School Of Fear
69. Symptoms of Witchcraft Attacks
70. Technical Prayers To Disgrace Local Goliath
71. The Dangerous Highway
72. The Enemy Has Done This

About The Book

It is here at last the deliverance manual for addressing dream battles and nightmares. By the time a person is 60 years old, he would have spent 20 years sleeping and dreaming. Your dreams are your spiritual monitoring system. Many do not know what is happening to their lives because, they do not understand their dreams. The land of slumber is as important as life itself.

Dreams from God are to: assure, encourage, comfort, direct, instruct, guide, exhort, correct, warn or reveal the plan and purposes of God.

Satanic dreams are noted for their absurdity, emptiness, harassment and punishment by dream criminals.

This book teaches you how to understand your dreams and how to deal with your dream battles. This book is a must for every serious Christian home. Read it and pray the prayer points therein and your life will no longer remain the same.

About BCCM, MFM Ministries and the Author

Dr. Daniel Kolawole Olukoya is the General Overseer of the Battle Cry Christian Ministries and Mountain of Fire and Miracles Ministries. The Mountain of Fire and Miracles Ministries' Headquarters in Lagos, Nigeria is the largest single Christian congregation in Africa with attendance of over 120,000 in single meetings.

MFM is a full gospel ministry devoted to the revival of Apostolic signs, Holy Ghost fireworks, miracles and the unlimited demonstration of the power of God to deliver to the uttermost. Absolute holiness within and without as the greatest spiritual insecticide and a pre-requisite for heaven is openly taught. MFM is a do-it-yourself gospel ministry, where your hands are trained to wage war and your fingers to do battle.

Dr. Olukoya holds a first class honours degree in Microbiology from the University of Lagos, Nigeria and a PhD in Molecular Genetics from the University of Reading, United Kingdom. As a researcher, he has over seventy scientific publications to his credit.

Anointed by God, Dr. D. K. Olukoya is a prophet, evangelist, teacher and preacher of the Word. His life and that of his wife, Shade and their son, Elijah Toluwani are living proofs that all power belongs to God.

The Battle Cry Christian Ministries is devoted to:
(a) teaching and disseminating information on Christian spiritual warfare,
(b) making available life-changing Christian articles and books at affordable prices and
(c) preparing an army of aggressive prayer warriors and intercessors in this end-time.

Published by:
The Battle Cry Christian Ministries
P. O. Box 12272, Ikeja, Tel/Fax 4939797, Lagos, Nigeria.

ISBN 978-35755-0-3

www.ingramcontent.com/pod-product-compliance
Lightning Source LLC
LaVergne TN
LVHW051225080426
835513LV00016B/1421